AF877109

Naval Leadership in Korea

The First Six Months

Thomas B. Buell

The U.S. Navy and the Korean War

Edward J. Marolda
Series Editor

Naval Historical Center
Department of the Navy
Washington 2002

Secretary of the Navy's
Advisory Subcommittee on Naval History

Dr. David Alan Rosenberg (Chair)
Commander Wesley A. Brown, CEC, USN (Ret.)
Dr. Frank G. Burke
Vice Admiral Robert F. Dunn, USN (Ret.)
Vice Admiral George W. Emery, USN (Ret.)
Dr. José-Marie Griffiths
Captain R. Robinson Harris, USN (Ret.)
Dr. Beverly Schreiber Jacoby
Rear Admiral John M. Kersh, USN (Ret.)
Dr. James R. Reckner
Dr. William N. Still Jr.
Ms. Virginia S. Wood

Cover design by Morgan I. Wilbur
Book design by John A Grier

Library of Congress Cataloging-in-Publication Data

Buell, Thomas B.
Naval leadership in Korea : the first six months / Thomas B. Buell
p. cm. — (The U.S. Navy and the Korean War)
Includes bibliographical references.
ISBN 0-945274-46-7 (alk. paper)
1. Korean War, 1950–1953—Naval operations, American. 2. United States. Navy—History. I. Title. II. Series.

DS920.A2 B84 2002
951.904'245—dc21 2001055890

∞ The paper used in this publication meets the requirements for permanence established by the American National Standard for Information Sciences "Permanence of Paper for Printed Library Materials" (ANSI Z39.48–1984).

For sale by the Superintendent of Documents, U.S. Government Printing Office
Internet: bookstore.gpo.gov Phone: toll free (866) 512-1800; DC area (202) 512-1800
Fax: (202) 512-2250 Mail: Stop SSOP, Washington, DC 20402-0001

ISBN 0-16-051080-5

To the Sailors who followed the naval leaders

NA 80-G-423716

Rear Admiral James H. Doyle awards the Silver Star decoration for bravery at Inchon to landing craft Sailors, left to right, Seaman Chancey H. Vogt, Seaman William H. Tagan, Engineman Fireman Richard P. Vinson, and Seaman Apprentice Paul J. Gregory.

Contents

Navy Art Collection, KN-13813

On the cover, Korean War naval leaders, right to left, Admiral Forrest P. Sherman, Chief of Naval Operations; Vice Admiral C. Turner Joy, Commander Naval Forces, Far East; and Rear Admiral Arleigh A. Burke, Joy's deputy chief of staff. Herbert C. Hahn's colored pencil drawing "A Hit" depicts a U.S. Navy battleship striking targets at Wonsan.

Foreword

THIS MONOGRAPH IS THE SECOND study in the Naval Historical Center's new series commemorating the 50th Anniversary of the Korean War. The series recognizes and remembers the contributions and sacrifices of our Sailors and Marines in the undeclared war on the Korean peninsula. While most monographs in the series focus on operational aspects of the war, *Naval Leadership in Korea* illuminates the role of the Navy's top flag officers in Washington, in the Pacific area, and in the Korean theater of operations before and during the first chaotic six months of war.

To set the stage, naval veteran and historian Thomas B. Buell describes the contentious post–World War II debates in Congress over the roles and missions of the services in our nation's national security. The future of the Navy's aircraft carrier arm remained uncertain after the establishment of an independent Air Force. The infighting between the Navy and the Air Force led to the firing of a Chief of Naval Operations and a public relations war that the Navy was losing. However, when North Korea invaded South Korea on 25 June 1950, the threat to carrier aviation quickly dissipated.

Thanks to the leadership of six influential naval officers, U.S. forces were mobilized and in South Korea within three weeks. During the remainder of that year, these six naval leaders interacted with their Marine, Army, and Air Force counterparts in the planning and successful execution of some of the most demanding operations of the Korean War.

We are grateful to Tom Buell for taking on the project and so ably setting the record straight on the complex command and control relationships wrought by the Korean War. His extensive use of oral histories brings to the reader an insider's view of the difficulties surrounding much of the operational planning in the early months. During that time, when staffs were limited and activity was high, these naval leaders also had to contend with operational restrictions imposed by the military chiefs and civilian leaders in Washington.

I wish to express my appreciation to Dr. Edward J. Marolda, the series editor, and to the Naval Historical Foundation, the Marine Corps History and Museums Division, and Lieutenant Colonel Ward E. Scott, USMC, Navy–Marine Corps Korean War Commemoration Coordinator, for their generous support that made the publication of this work possible. As with all the works in the series, the views expressed are those of the author and do not necessarily reflect those of the Department of the Navy or any other U.S. government agency.

William S. Dudley
Director of Naval History

Preface

WHEN DR. EDWARD J. MAROLDA of the Naval Historical Center invited me to write about naval leaders of the Korean War, I gladly assented. The experience was challenging and interesting for me, as I had only a basic knowledge of the war and its naval leaders. For example, I knew C. Turner Joy largely as the chief negotiator at the armistice talks, and as a very tired and subdued superintendent of the U.S. Naval Academy during my plebe year. I knew nothing of his accomplishments as Commander Naval Forces, Far East. Similarly, James Doyle was just a name and a picture. I knew he was the principal amphibious commander in the early months of the war, but not much more. I now realize those two men were chiefly responsible for preventing the defeat of United Nations forces in the first six months of the war.

As this work is intended as a monograph, I necessarily had to limit its scope. I decided upon the first six months of war ending on 31 December 1950, the period of the most intense and decisive naval operations. Other monographs in the series will address naval activities during the remainder of the war.

While there were many distinguished naval leaders in this period, I could not write about them all, so I chose six protagonists who were intimately involved in the strategy, planning, and execution of the most critical operations. They are Admiral Forrest P. Sherman, Chief of Naval Operations; Admiral Arthur W. Radford, Commander in Chief, Pacific and Commander in Chief, Pacific Fleet; Vice Admiral C. Turner Joy, Commander Naval Forces, Far East; Vice Admiral Arthur D. Struble, Commander Seventh Fleet and Commander Joint Task Force 7; Rear Admiral James H. Doyle, Commander Task Force 90 and Commander Amphibious Group 1; and Rear Admiral Arleigh A. Burke, Deputy Chief of Staff, Naval Forces, Far East.

I have focused on the command relationships among these six men, and their interaction with Marine, Army, and Air Force leaders. The war followed immediately after the bitter service unification hearings of the late 1940s in which Sherman, Radford, Struble, and Burke had all been intimately involved at one time or another. Now, in this extraordinary national emergency, past animosities had to be put aside so that the services could pull together. It would not be easy.

I have discovered and provided herein new information not in the literature and have refrained from covering operational details published elsewhere. To the point, I focused on the preludes to the operations rather than the operations themselves, emphasizing the influence each of the six protagonists exerted on the way things were to be done. The reader will discover, as I did, that the protagonists often disagreed with their Army and Air Force colleagues, and among themselves, and that relations were often antagonistic regardless of uniform. They were, after all, human, with egos and prejudices that influenced behavior and relationships. But their professionalism transcended personalities. These were the naval leaders who turned back the invaders.

I want to express my gratitude to those who helped me, beginning with two historians at the

Naval Historical Center, Ed Marolda and Dr. Jeffrey G. Barlow. Ed got me started, freely gave me sound advice, edited the manuscript, and produced the final monograph. Jeff's fine work, *Revolt of the Admirals,* was the source for my introduction; moreover, he wisely suggested that I contact Don Chisholm, an expert on the amphibious aspects of the Korean War. Don stimulated my thinking with his paper "Negotiated Joint Command Relationships: Korean War Amphibious Operations, 1950" in the *Naval War College Review* (Spring 2000), and he generously shared his extensive collection of research materials that saved me weeks of work in scattered archives. Dr. David Alan Rosenberg, the biographer of Arleigh Burke, copied hundreds of microfilm "Blue Flag" messages for my use and expedited their declassification. Paul Stillwell and Ann Hassinger at the U.S. Naval Institute opened that organization's oral history collection for my needs and provided materials from the Institute's archives.

I also wish to thank the Naval Historical Foundation, which generously supported my research.

Finally, I wish to thank my readers, Jim Abrahamson, Don Chisholm, and my wife, Marilyn, for their perceptive comments and suggestions.

Thomas B. Buell

Prologue

IT WAS THE STRANGEST of all naval wars, if it could even be called a naval war, for a naval war has opposing navies. The United States Navy in Korea was unopposed by a conventional enemy navy. Five years before the shooting started in Korea, the United States was the world's greatest sea power, having defeated the Axis powers, a victory culminating in the surrender ceremony on board USS *Missouri* in Tokyo Bay. The Navy then had some 68,000 vessels of all types on hand and over four million people—Sailors, Marines, and Coastguardsmen—in uniform. The postwar demobilization left the naval service with but a remnant of its wartime strength, and the Truman administration intended to emasculate it yet further.

By limiting appropriations in peacetime, American politicians had managed to devastate the naval service as had no enemy in war. They acted neither for vengeance nor for want of gratitude for the victory in World War II, but because they could perceive no need for a navy in the circumstances of the late 1940s. The Soviet Union was a looming threat to the security of the free world, but the U.S. Air Force had argued convincingly that its long-range bombers and atomic bombs were the primary deterrents to Soviet aggression. As the Soviet Union was then a land power with a negligible navy, conventional wisdom reasoned that the U.S. Navy would have no great role in the event of war on the continent.

The naval establishment had blundered by not making its case and by allowing the Air Force to define the terms of the acrimonious roles-and-missions debates in Congress, the Pentagon, and the press. Ostensibly, armed forces unification was the overriding interservice quarrel—the Navy was against it, the Air Force and Army were for it. The root of the dispute, however, was whose aircraft would do what. Flag officers like Vice Admiral Arthur W. Radford, Vice Chief of Naval Operations (VCNO), argued that the aircraft carrier had been proven in war as the core of sea power. Thus when the Air Force argued that the B-36 intercontinental bomber made the aircraft carrier redundant, and that in any event an atomic bomb would sink a fleet in an instant, the Navy was stung and came out swinging. The Navy-Air Force brawl became predicated upon a single issue: which system—carrier or bomber—was best suited to drop atomic bombs on Russia?

By advocating that the carrier's (ergo the Navy's) primary mission should be strategic bombing, and that it could do it better than the B-36, the Navy adopted a narrow, all-or-nothing argument. If it lost that argument, it would lose everything, for no other plausible justification for the Navy's existence was forthcoming. And lose that argument it surely would, owing to the Navy's long-standing ineptness in public relations and its inability to justify itself.

Other arguments rarely materialized. Control of the sea, the once traditional role of the Navy, now seemed irrelevant in the absence of any other sea power. When in his ignorance General of the Army Omar N. Bradley, chairman of the Joint Chiefs of Staff (JCS), shrilly dismissed the Marine Corps and amphibious warfare as wholly unnecessary in any future war, the Navy did not respond.

NA USAF K-4823

The Joint Chiefs of Staff meet in 1948 after discussions on service roles and missions with Secretary of Defense James V. Forrestal: Left to right, General Hoyt S. Vandenberg, Chief of Staff, U.S. Air Force; Admiral Louis E. Denfeld, Chief of Naval Operations, and General Omar N. Bradley, Chief of Staff, U.S. Army.

To be convincing in political and public forums required officers to present articulate, well-thought-out arguments, but the Navy Department in the late 1940s suffered from an intellectual vacuum. Flag officers then leading the Navy had made their number during World War II and had learned by doing. Hence, there evolved among many of them an institutional disdain for war college training and the associated disciplines of sound reasoning, abstract thought, and verbal clarity. Things learned in the school of the ship were of little value in Washington, and as a consequence, the Navy floundered when confronting Air Force propaganda.

In countering the Army-Air Force public relations campaign for unification of the services, the Navy first relied upon a group of OPNAV officers known as the Secretary's Committee on Research and Reorganization (SCOROR), established in late 1945 and initially headed by Vice Admiral Radford, then Deputy Chief of Naval Operations (DCNO) for Air. As the Navy's principal proponent for naval air power and for preserving the independence of the naval service, Radford fiercely opposed nearly every unification scheme proposed by the Army and its allies. Although a shrewd, persuasive bureaucrat skilled in the give and take of Washington politics, Radford achieved only limited successes on behalf of the Navy Department. He became so strongly identified as a foe of unification and Air Force aspirations that his opponents wished him out of Washington.

He left for a time to command the Second Fleet but returned in January 1948 to serve as Vice Chief of Naval Operations, a tour that lasted 18 months. Louis E. Denfeld, a submariner, had just been appointed Chief of Naval Operations (CNO), and he told the Chief of Naval Personnel that he wanted "an aviator who had the complete confidence of Naval aviators, both young and old, one who had a good war record and one who would be completely loyal in working out the unification legislation as it affects the Navy." After returning to Washington, Radford resumed his struggles against the Air Force and President Harry S. Truman's relentless whittling of the strength of the armed services.

Meanwhile the Secretary of the Navy's Committee on Unification (UNICOM) had replaced SCOROR, functioning since June 1948 as the coordinating agency for "unification problems relative to Navy basic concepts, doctrines and policies." Still the Navy continued to sustain losses to the smooth-talking Air Force spokesmen. Recognizing the sterility of UNICOM, Secretary of the Navy John L. Sullivan dissolved it seven months after it had been established.

Sullivan, Denfeld, and Marine Commandant General Clifton B. Cates discussed what, or who, would replace UNICOM. Two imperatives occupied their attention. First, unification strategy had to be coherent and coordinated to ensure the Navy's independence, if not its survival. Second, naval policies had to be developed that would be universally supported within the service. As the so-called revolt of the admirals concerned solely aviation, surface and submarine officers felt that their interests were being disregarded. Moreover, bungling leadership exacerbated the unbroken unification disasters that demoralized and humiliated the naval officer corps as an institution. Sullivan, Denfeld, and Cates were on the spot, and as one observer described it, "[T]hey were determined that something had to be done to get the Navy back into believing in itself."

Despite all the flag officers at its disposal, the high command chose a captain, Arleigh A. Burke, to act as the Navy's brainpower. Burke was a famous surface warrior who had served as chief of staff to one of the Navy's greatest aviators, Marc Mitscher. Hence, Burke was persona grata to both the surface and aviation communities, the "black shoes" and the "brown shoes." Furthermore, Burke had served on the General Board after the war and demonstrated an extraordinary intellectual capacity to think, analyze, reason, and write on great and complex issues. Summoned to Washington from his cruiser command on Christmas Day 1948, Burke learned he was about to undertake a potentially career-ending assignment on the unification battlefield. There was the likelihood that the Truman administration, the Office of the Secretary of Defense, and the Air Force would consider him an enemy, that the press would portray him as acting with intrigue and duplicity, and that special interests in the Navy might deem him disloyal if he proposed unpopular policies.

Taking such hazards in stride and pressing on, Burke took charge of OP-23, titled the Organizational Research and Policy Division in the Office of the Chief of Naval Operations. But developments beyond Burke's control continued to rock a Navy in distress. Louis A. Johnson replaced the ailing James Forrestal as Secretary of Defense on 28 March 1949. Less than a month later Johnson cancelled construction of the new carrier USS *United States*. The Air Force rejoiced. Secretary Sullivan resigned in protest.

◆ ◆ ◆

For political reasons Johnson wanted a prominent Roman Catholic layman as Sullivan's replacement. Francis P. Matthews was that and little more. His religion being sufficient unto itself and unburdened with either relevant skills or experience, Matthews was sworn in as the new Navy secretary on 25 May 1949. Naval officers soon loathed him because of his subservience to Johnson and his hostility to their interests. Internal turmoil intensified, and the Navy's decline accelerated. A hostile leak infuriated Matthews, and he suspected that Burke's shop, with intent to embarrass him, was the source. Matthews ordered the Inspector General to impound OP-23's files, but nothing incriminating was discovered. Nonetheless, a vengeful Matthews attempted, unsuccessfully, to stymie Burke's selection to rear admiral.

Meanwhile congressional hearings went on, and the naval aviators led by Radford (by then a full

NA USAF K-5155

The newly appointed Secretary of Defense, Louis A. Johnson, meets with his service secretaries: Left to right, W. Stuart Symington, Secretary of the Air Force; Kenneth C. Royall, Secretary of the Army; Johnson; and John L. Sullivan, Secretary of the Navy. In less than a month, Johnson's actions would prompt Sullivan to resign.

NA 111-C-5848

At age 53, Admiral Forrest P. Sherman became the youngest Chief of Naval Operations, serving in the Navy's highest leadership position from November 1949 to July 1951, when he died of a heart attack.

admiral in command of the Pacific Command and the Pacific Fleet) decried the B-36. To Matthews' dismay, Denfeld testified that the aviators were right and that, by implication, Matthews was wrong—since Matthews' own testimony had portrayed the aviators as a cabal without support by the Navy's rank and file. Matthews and Johnson subsequently fired Denfeld for testifying to what he believed. The Navy cheered Denfeld for his act of self-immolation.

Whoever relieved Denfeld as CNO would have to resolve the ethical conflict between obedience to hostile civilian authority and loyalty to a naval service dissatisfied with that authority. Presumably Johnson and Matthews wanted someone who would enforce Johnson's intentions, namely not to build a new carrier, to reduce the size of the Navy, and to avoid further opposition to the B-36 program. Any such officer would, of course, be considered a betrayer by his colleagues.

Vice Admiral Forrest P. Sherman, thought by many to be overly ambitious, was willing and available. He commanded the Sixth Fleet in the Mediterranean and,

> "I guess Forrest Sherman is down there telling them everything they want to hear."
>
> —Admiral Louis E. Denfeld

although a naval aviator, figuratively and literally, had stood clear of the mud-slinging B-36 hearings. Thus, in Matthews' mind he was not one of *them*. Sherman was universally recognized as an intellectual and a planner, and as a staff officer he had been close to Nimitz. When Nimitz became CNO, Sherman followed him to Washington as his DCNO for Operations. There he undertook the difficult job of representing the Navy in negotiations culminating in an agreement on unification, which in turn became the basis for the National Security Act of 1947. The act created an independent Air Force and a Secretary of Defense who presided over a unified National Military Establishment. Predictably Sherman's role was resented within the Navy, but with Nimitz as his mentor and the White House giving its approval Sherman's career path remained unimpeded.

Matthews summoned Sherman from the Mediterranean for consultations without telling Denfeld. Under normal circumstances Sherman would have made a courtesy call on Denfeld; moreover, by protocol only the CNO directed flag officers to come to Washington. But in this instance Sherman avoided Denfeld altogether. The embittered CNO confided to aides, "I guess Forrest Sherman is down there telling them everything they want to hear."

Viewed as an opportunist by a good portion of the naval establishment, Sherman was announced as the new CNO on 1 November 1949, at 53 the youngest officer ever to hold the post. Sherman quickly abolished OP-23.

◆◆◆

Months earlier Radford had gotten his fourth star and gone to Pearl Harbor to command the remnants of the once-mighty Pacific Fleet. He had returned to Washington temporarily to testify in the October 1949 B-36 hear-

NA 80-G-706108

In its roles and missions debate with the Air Force, the Navy lost the funding for its newly designed super carrier United States, *seen in this conceptual drawing. A few days after the carrier's keel laying at Newport News Shipbuilding, Secretary of Defense Louis Johnson cancelled its construction.*

USN 625685

President Truman appointed Francis P. Matthews as Secretary of the Navy after John Sullivan resigned. Naval officers regarded Matthews with distain because he often ignored their interests and sided with Defense Secretary Johnson in naval matters.

ings, but he had been the last strong spokesman for naval air. The aviators despaired when Vice Admiral Arthur D. Struble, DCNO for Operations, became by default the principal naval representative in the development of military policy with the JCS. As a black shoe, he was not one of the club, and he avoided disputes. Those still fighting the problem desired him out of Washington, and they wanted Denfeld to assign him to command of the Seventh Fleet in the far-off Western Pacific in the summer of 1949. "He can't do us any harm there," remarked one critic.

By August Denfeld had not acted, so Struble remained in Washington, in the eyes of the aviators, hurting their cause. In an exchange of letters with another senior aviator, Radford wrote:

> Struble has done more harm to the Navy in the time he has been there than anyone else could have possibly done. I discussed this with Louis [Denfeld] before I left in April, and at that time Louis assured me that he would appoint a separate JCS assistant. . . . If Struble were relieved of his contacts with the JCS he could not do much damage—although I would favor getting him completely out of the operations picture.

In all likelihood Denfeld retained Struble for reasons of continuity, and certainly he was the kind of staff officer that Sherman wanted when he became CNO in November 1949. In mid-1950 Sherman did indeed send Struble to command the Seventh Fleet, but as a normal rotation and not as an exile. He would report to Radford, who distrusted him.

In many ways, the confrontation between the Air Force and the Navy that involved Sherman, Radford, and Struble, and the disagreements among these naval flag officers, prepared them for the exacting task of leading U.S. naval forces during the chaotic first six months of the Korean War.

The Inspector-General's Raid

The Air Force's B-36 intercontinental bomber was at the crux of the bitter argument between the Navy and the Air Force over the mission of dropping bombs on targets in the Soviet Union.

COMMANDER SNOWDEN Arthur, a member of the OP-23 (Organizational Research and Policy Division) staff, periodically cruised by the CNO's office to hear the latest rumors from a friendly lieutenant. It was late afternoon, 29 September 1949. The lieutenant had startling news. "They're gonna raid you," he warned. "The IG's headed toward you." Alarmed, Arthur scurried to Rear Admiral Arleigh Burke's office. Burke said he did not know why he was being targeted, but in any event there were files he did not want discovered. Opening file drawers, he and Arthur immediately began to stash papers into a briefcase.

Shortly, Rear Admiral Allan R. McCann, the Inspector General, entered Burke's office. Marine staff officer Lieutenant Colonel Samuel R. Shaw saw the expression on McCann's face. "You looked at that man," he recalled, "and you knew something was afoot." Arthur stood frozen with briefcase in hand in the next room as McCann confronted Burke. "Arleigh, it's a raid," he said coldly. "I want to talk to you in the hall." Burke and McCann went out and closed the entryway door. "I took off like a catapult," Arthur recalled, one step ahead of McCann's Marine sentries who minutes later closed every exit. In a nearby office, he found a friend who agreed to put the briefcase in his safe, and he then went home.

While Burke and McCann were outside, Shaw talked with staff officer Commander Joseph L. Howard about the probable reasons for the IG raid. The Navy's top flag officers were preparing to testify before the House Armed Services Committee, which had held hearings that allowed the Air Force to promote successfully the B-36 program, hearings which coincidentally had greatly embarrassed the Navy. Despite Air Force protests, the Navy (but not Secretary of the Navy Francis Matthews) wanted to testify in rebuttal, ostensibly to advocate the need for aircraft carriers. Just before the hearings were to begin, Matthews had ordered the admirals not to bring up the B-36. Recoiling, they protested that the Air Force had made claims that had to be challenged. The next morning an article in the *Washington Post* charged that Matthews had muzzled the witnesses. While in reality VCNO John Dale Price had leaked the story, an enraged Matthews suspected Burke and had sent the IG to investigate. Rear Admiral Howard recalled the incident: "Sam Shaw seemed to sense, right away, what it was all about. I didn't, but Sam Shaw did. And he and I—just the two of us—began frantically to adjust our files and make damn sure that if they were gonna go through the files that there would be some things that they wouldn't be able to find."

As additional IG people surrounded the OP-23 offices, McCann told Burke to order his staff to remain in their offices and to recall those who had left. Burke could scarcely restrain his fury, but at his direction the entire staff was assembled and confined to their offices into the night. One by one they were taken to the IG offices for interrogation. Burke was the first to be summoned.

The IG interrogators were severe and intimidating but did not reveal the purpose of the investigation. Shaw remembered it was like being questioned in a police station. Their questions largely centered on office routine and contacts with the press, leading some of the staff to suspect that the morning's *Washington Post* article was the cause. As no one in Burke's office had leaked the article, it was foreordained that McCann would find no evidence, but the process reduced all of the staffers to nervous exhaustion. McCann concluded his investigation in the early hours of the morning, dismissing Burke's staff with a warning to say nothing of what had happened.

Burke had dodged the bullet.

North Korea Attacks

Admiral, the Navy is on its way out. . . . There's no reason for having a Navy and Marine Corps. General Bradley tells me that amphibious operations are a thing of the past. We'll never have any more amphibious operations. That does away with the Marine Corps. And the Air Force can do anything the Navy can nowadays, so that does away with the Navy.

—Secretary of Defense Louis A. Johnson to Admiral Richard L. Conolly, December 1949

REAR ADMIRAL JAMES H. Doyle was a master practitioner of amphibious warfare. He had seen it all during World War II. He had been Admiral Richmond Kelly Turner's operations officer during the Guadalcanal and Solomons campaigns, when the Navy was first learning amphibious warfare by trial and error. In the latter part of the war, when amphibious ships had numbered in the thousands, Doyle was a principal amphibious planner on Admiral Ernest J. King's staff in Washington. After a postwar hiatus he returned to the "alligator navy" in 1948. For two years he commanded the Amphibious Training Command in Coronado, California, keeping alive a form of warfare derided as obsolete by many in the Air Force and Army. Absorbed in the disagreements with the Air Force over aviation matters, even the Navy had given low priority to its amphibious capability. Because the Marines were fighting to survive against an antagonistic president, it was questionable whether the Navy would even have a landing force.

Doyle finally got to fly his flag at sea when he took command of Amphibious Group (PHIBGRP) 1 in January 1950. A vestige of a once mighty naval force, PHIBGRP 1 comprised but five ships, one of each type: a flagship (AGC), an attack transport (APA), an attack cargo ship (AKA), a tank landing ship (LST), and a fleet tug (ATF). No one ventured to say exactly what it was expected to do as the Navy retrenched in the aftermath of the unification fight. Perhaps this was Doyle's twilight cruise. Since he was in the Navy's backwater force, a promotion to vice admiral seemed unlikely. It might be time for him to think of retirement and a new career, for he was also a lawyer.

In the spring an unexpected summons came from Douglas MacArthur, Commander in Chief, Far East (CINCFE). The general had let it be known that he wanted amphibious training for his army occupation forces in Japan. Ecstatic that a senior Army officer of MacArthur's prestige still felt that the Navy's amphibious forces were useful, the Navy sent Doyle and his ships to Japan. It was a logical and fortuitous decision: Doyle was accustomed to conducting amphibious training and had already embarked Marines from the Troop Training Unit, Coronado. They would train MacArthur's army. No other ships were available

NA 80-G-427790

Vice Admiral C. Turner Joy was one of the most powerful and influential naval officers of the Korean War. He commanded and controlled all naval forces in the Korean theater and represented Navy and Marine interests within General MacArthur's headquarters. He strongly influenced MacArthur's decision to keep UN forces on the Korean peninsula during the Chinese attack of December 1950.

in mine warfare. Few other flag officers were more qualified to lead the naval forces in the war that was about to erupt.

It was America's good fortune that when Joy and Doyle sat over coffee, the Navy had put in place the two naval officers whose presence would be instrumental in preventing North Korea from taking and occupying South Korea by armed aggression. Yet, they were there not because of any prescience in the Navy Department, but because of MacArthur's understanding of the Navy's worth. CIA intelligence reports and his own staff had been predicting war in June. While MacArthur entertained doubts that Truman would allow the United States to become involved, he nonetheless could take measures to be prepared. Publicly, however, MacArthur predicted a status quo in the Far East.

in the entire Pacific Fleet, so pitiably few were the numbers of amphibious vessels in commission.

When he arrived in Japan in late June, Doyle called on Vice Admiral C. Turner Joy, Commander Naval Forces, Far East (COMNAVFE), whose office was down the street from MacArthur's Tokyo headquarters. A decorated warrior, Joy had commanded a cruiser and later a cruiser division during several of the greatest battles of the Pacific war. When the war ended, he was commanding an amphibious group preparing for the invasion of Japan. Before and after the war he had operated in Far Eastern waters and was intimately familiar with both the Chinese and the China coast. He was also an ordnance and gunnery specialist with special expertise

Admiral Forrest P. Sherman (left), Chief of Naval Operations, and Admiral Arthur W. Radford, Commander in Chief, Pacific, in July 1950, discuss the grim news from the Far East where Communist forces threatened to push the allies off the Korean peninsula.

NA 80-G-427791

Admirals Sherman and Radford prepare to discuss the Korean situation at a press briefing of July 1950 in San Diego.

Still, his asking for amphibious training for his soldiers was not a whim. MacArthur's request had to have been deliberate and his thinking alone, for few on his staff had an inkling of the capabilities and intricacies of amphibious warfare. Had MacArthur not done so when he did, Doyle and his ships would have been in San Diego when the North Koreans attacked, and MacArthur would have been without means to get his troops from Japan to the Korean peninsula. North Korea would have occupied all of South Korea within weeks. Indeed, had Doyle not been in Japan, it is possible that Truman would not have ordered MacArthur to send troops into Korea, for certainly Sherman would have told the President there were no ships available. As we shall see, Doyle got the 1st Cavalry Division into Korea in the nick of time.

The fact that the Naval Forces, Far East command even existed was because MacArthur wanted naval ships under his direct control as CINCFE. While the Navy considered it as no more than a minor naval force to aid MacArthur in his occupation duties in Japan, the naval service ensured that a vice admiral was in command. Washington was determined that the ranking naval officer under MacArthur would wear the same three stars as MacArthur's senior Army and Air Force generals. As a matter of courtesy it would also have been customary for the Navy to have MacArthur's approval of Joy's assignment before cutting his orders. All in all MacArthur had good relations with the Navy; flag officers who knew him liked him, and he treated the Navy well.

Joy had a cruiser, four destroyers, and six minesweepers under his command, but a rear admiral looked after them as they undertook such nominal tasks as antismuggling patrols and showing the flag. His staff of 29 officers and 160 enlisted men was organized for such peacetime administrative functions as coordinating Japanese-manned minesweepers clearing mines laid around the Home Islands during the war, facilitating the restoration of the Japanese merchant marine and shipbuilding industries, and supervising the naval stations at Yokosuka and Sasebo. The staff was neither organized nor prepared for a wartime emergency.

Joy and Doyle were old friends, so they quickly resumed their amiable relationship. When they went to MacArthur's headquarters, soon after Doyle's arrival in Japan, they encountered Secretary Johnson and General Bradley, who were touring the Far East. Bradley asked what Doyle was doing there.

"I am here," Doyle replied, "to give amphibious training to units of the Eighth Army at General MacArthur's request."

Bradley looked scornfully at Doyle and said nothing.

Doyle told MacArthur of the encounter, associating it with Bradley's earlier prediction that amphibious warfare was passé.

It was MacArthur's turn to be scornful: "Bradley is a farmer."

Doyle had agreeable memories of his first contact with MacArthur when both were in the Philippines before the war. He was pleased to see MacArthur once again, although he doubted that the general remembered him. MacArthur greeted Doyle warmly and explained his expectations for the training that Doyle had steamed the breadth of the Pacific to provide.

MacArthur's soldiers, the 35th Regimental Combat Team, first assembled with Doyle's training team on 25 June. The exercise was cancelled when word was received of the North Korea attack. Doyle went on 4-hour standby, anticipating orders.

◆ ◆ ◆

Struble was in Washington on 25 June, and his first reaction was to return to his diminutive "fleet"—its combatants were one carrier, a cruiser, eight destroyers, and four submarines—then in the Philippines and Hong Kong. Sherman told him to wait until after the CNO and the JCS met with Truman and his civilian advisors. The next day Sherman told Struble that American forces would be committed to Korea, although to what extent remained to be determined. Initially Washington authorized only such military action as was necessary to evacuate and protect Americans then in South Korea, and Secretary of State Dean Acheson warned that Korea might be a feint to mask a Chinese invasion of Taiwan and a Russian invasion of Europe. Whatever the Navy's eventual employment, Struble, as he returned to his command, knew the Seventh Fleet would be part of it.

> "I am here to give amphibious training to units of the Eighth Army at General MacArthur's request."
>
> —Rear Admiral James H. Doyle

Meanwhile General Clifton B. Cates, Commandant of the Marine Corps, was puzzled about how his Marines would be used. Secretary Matthews cancelled his regular conferences, and neither Matthews nor Sherman would grant Cates an audience. The general was convinced that the cold shoulder was intentional and that the administration meant to exclude the Marines from fighting in Korea, and he was not surprised. He had become accustomed to slurs and rebuffs. Truman was an avowed opponent of the Corps, and Bradley wanted to eliminate the Marines altogether.

By chance Sherman and Cates met in a Pentagon corridor on 29 June. Cates observed that things were looking grim. Sherman agreed.

"Why doesn't MacArthur ask for Marines?" asked Cates.

"What do you have?" Sherman replied.

Cates explained that he could immediately mount a provisional brigade comprising a regimental combat team and a Marine air group from the 1st Marine Division at Camp Pendleton.

"Leave it to me," said Sherman after a pause. "I'll send a Blue Flag message to Joy."

Cates was puzzled for he had never heard of the private communication channel used by the Navy's senior flag officers. Several days passed until, on 3 July, Cates heard that, thanks to Joy's advocacy, MacArthur had requested the Marine brigade Cates had offered, and that the JCS would discuss it shortly. Cates went to Sherman and insisted that he be allowed to attend the meeting. The JCS reluctantly allowed him in, but agreed to send the Marines. Cates regarded the JCS decision as grudging because he felt they wanted to keep the Marines out of the war. Eventually MacArthur pounded on the JCS until it agreed to send the entire 1st Marine Division for the invasion of Inchon.

"China Seas" by combat artist Herbert Hahn. Rough weather failed to slow Task Force 77 as it steamed to the Korean combat area.

"Sherman didn't like the Marines," Cates later said, "but he was fair and square."

After Denfeld had been fired, Cates told Matthews that he hoped he wasn't considering Sherman as the new CNO. Matthews did not respond. The next day Sherman's appointment was announced.

"You certainly weren't my candidate," Cates told Sherman soon afterward.

"Well general," Sherman replied, "every man is entitled to his opinion."

◆ ◆ ◆

Admiral Arthur W. Radford, Commander in Chief, Pacific, and Commander in Chief, Pacific Fleet, later recalled that he had gotten everything steaming westward as soon as he had heard about the attack in Korea. He pondered his and the Navy's role in the developing war, for it was unsettling that decisions from Washington seemed reluctant and hesitant and that forces were being committed piecemeal. Moreover, Radford was aware of the institutional hostility of the Office of the Secretary of Defense and the Army and Air Force members of the JCS toward the Navy and Marine Corps. He was also aware that the JCS, and especially the Army, were worried about a war in Europe and concerned that Korea was a diversion. In an early meeting with MacArthur he saw General J. Lawton Collins, Chief of Staff of the Army, tell MacArthur he would have to win the war with the troops available to him in Japan and Korea. MacArthur smiled. "Joe," he said, "you are going to have to change your mind."

Later MacArthur privately asked Radford what he thought the Marines might be able to contribute. A brigade almost immediately, Radford replied, and probably a full division by fall. MacArthur was already thinking about Inchon.

Realizing that Sherman was the voice of one crying in the wilderness, Radford wanted to give him some ammunition. Hence, once the JCS had told MacArthur to fight the North Korean People's Army (NKPA), Radford counseled Sherman on 8 July in a way that reflected Radford's wisdom and broad strategic view, foretelling his eventual elevation to the JCS chairmanship. "I feel it is my duty," he wired Sherman, "to submit the following for your consideration in regard to my support of [MacArthur]."

> Over two thirds of the ships in the Pacific Fleet are either directly supporting [MacArthur] or are committed to his support. The remainder of my command is being made ready as quickly as possible to assist [MacArthur] as required. However, for the following reasons, the forces available in the Pacific Fleet are insufficient to provide the support which I believe is urgently required:
>
> The initial effects of the surprise attack on South Korea was countered to some extent by the resistance of South Korea and the surprise of the communists at the decision of the United States to fight if necessary to hold this area. The forces available to [MacArthur] are limited and known to the communists. The forces in North Korea are greater in number and the reserve of Chinese communists in South Manchuria are reported to be about 200,000 troops, at least part of which can be moved to the battle area.
>
> I consider that the importance of Korea to the communists (and the effect of its loss on U.S. prestige in the world) will require them to make every effort with the forces available in that area to defeat the U.S. forces. The United States cannot hope to hold Korea by number of troops but must depend upon mobility, mechanized forces, training and superiority of naval and air power at the point of conflict. I believe that the communists will

Blue Flag Messages

THE PROLIFERATION OF Top Secret messages particularly stressed communications resources, because just a handful of people on communications staffs had Top Secret clearance. Only they could encrypt, decrypt, and route the flood of classified traffic, and the procedures were tedious. Before the Korean War Top Secret messages were a rarity; now they had become commonplace. A special Top Secret message category, called Blue Flag, which had been established solely for private communication among a small circle of flag officers, quickly began getting a lot of use. Not even Secretary of the Navy Francis Matthews was aware of their existence, nor were general officers of the other services. (The Blue Flag term referred to the traditional blue flags flown by Navy admirals.)

As the war entered its sixth month in December 1950, the Secretary's aide Captain Harry B. Temple spilled the beans to Matthews. Temple told Matthews he had drafted Blue Flags while he was in the Far East and was presumptuous enough to tell Matthews that he should see them. It was an embarrassing and awkward revelation that CNO Forrest P. Sherman and his admirals had a private line that excluded Matthews, who naturally presumed he should know everything known by the admirals. When he asked Sherman for an explanation, the CNO agreed to show Matthews personally, "such Blue Flags as are appropriate." Moreover, Sherman ordered Radford and Joy to reduce the Blue Flags to a minimum and ensure that only flag officers drafted them, in effect closing the barn door. Nonetheless, Top Secret messages flowed unabated, though fewer were Blue Flags.

After the war, the CNO's Top Secret message files were preserved on microfilm reels. Presumably, the orginials were destroyed after the microfilming. Until recently the microfilm files remained classified and unavailable to historians. The standard Navy Department reason for refusing to declassify the Blue Flags was that retired senior flag officers did not want their private thoughts and communications to become public knowledge. In the late 1950s, the Director of Naval History contracted with James A. Field to write an official history of United States naval operations in Korea. As Field wrote in his explanation of source materials:

> The principal lacuna in the naval sources, and one that is reflected in the narrative, concerns the control and direction of the naval campaign. For Korea, as for the Second World War, information on such evanescent matters as the availability of intelligence, estimates of the situation, concepts of employment of own forces, and relations with the other services and with allies, must be sought in the dispatch traffic between the flag officers involved [i.e., Blue Flag]. But this remains an unexplored field. Although the availability of all pertinent naval sources was a condition of my undertaking this history, I have been unable to gain access to this material.

The Navy had denied Field access to all material classified higher than Secret. By good fortune and the good offices of naval historians, the Navy Department declassified some of the Blue Flag files and made them available for this publication on naval leadership. Work is under way to review the entire microfilm collection for declassification.

continue to depend upon a superior number of troops, the mechanized equipment available in the general area, limited available air support and USSR advisors to the North Korean forces. Time and distance are on the side of the communists. We must make the most effective measures immediately to back up our presently committed forces. If we do not, we may ultimately be defeated in that area.

I believe that the American public will support any measures which may be required to insure victory in Korea. They have been told that new weapons and new methods of delivery will insure U.S. superiority in any area and their reaction should the U.S. be driven out of Korea would be great.

I recommend that immediate steps be taken to provide [MacArthur] with additional ground forces and air forces of the types needed for close air support [i.e., Navy and Marine aircraft]. That additional amphibious and other shipping be activated to carry and logistically supply these forces; that additional ships and aircraft squadrons . . . be activated in order to provide adequate naval support; that the presently committed Marine [provisional brigade] be built up to full division strength as soon as practicable. Detailed recommendations for additional naval strength will follow by separate dispatch.

◆ ◆ ◆

Meanwhile in Japan, Joy had conferred with MacArthur. Both were surprised that Truman intended to fight the North Koreans, although the rules of engagement were obscure and would remain so. MacArthur was also miffed that Washington had not consulted him beforehand. So unexpected was the attack and Truman's response to it that MacArthur and Joy had no contingency plans whatsoever. Accustomed to sleepy administrative tasks, Joy's staff was jolted overnight into emergency wartime planning for which it was wholly unprepared.

The most immediate question facing Joy was command and control of naval forces in the Far East. Any ship operating in Korean, Chinese, or Taiwanese waters would be in MacArthur's theater and hence under his unified command. This was a radical departure from the World War II arrangements, for Fleet Admiral King had never allowed the fast carriers to fall under MacArthur's direct control. During the Leyte campaign the lack of a unified command and the poor liaison between Admiral William F. Halsey and Vice Admiral Thomas C. Kinkaid, commanding the Third and Seventh Fleets respectively, had endangered the amphibious shipping in Leyte Gulf. Halsey had commanded the fast carriers of the Third Fleet covering the amphibious assault and had reported to Nimitz; MacArthur had no say in their employment. Kinkaid, who reported to MacArthur, commanded the amphibious shipping and the close support warships. Consequently, Halsey had a free hand to do as he pleased and left the beachhead unprotected to chase a distant decoy force. A Japanese surface force entered the gulf and would have fallen on the transports had not the escort carriers and destroyers of Kinkaid's Seventh Fleet put up enough of a fight to discourage the enemy's advance.

This magnitude of split naval responsibility would not be repeated in Korea. (Although to a much lesser extent, personalities made the Navy command structure a contentious issue. Joy did his best to mediate and promote harmony such that, whatever the degree of naval command discord, it did not affect the Navy's performance at Inchon and Wonsan. In contrast, the appalling lack of a unified Army command and dispersion of forces on the Korean peninsula would complicate operations when the Chinese Army attacked.) The JCS had some time earlier agreed that the Seventh Fleet would be placed under MacArthur's control in the event of an emergency in his area. Two days after the war began, Radford accordingly ordered Struble and his Seventh Fleet (centered around its fast carrier) to report to Joy for operational control. Since Joy reported to MacArthur, the general now had direct control—exercised through Joy—over the employment of the carriers. By fait accompli, Struble would report to Joy for orders, but as he was senior to Joy, a sacrosanct naval precedent was disregarded. Seniors normally did not report to juniors. In this instance there was no choice.

Joy's first order to Struble was to steam for Okinawa, for he had learned that the Seventh Fleet was headed to Sasebo, Japan, within range of Russian air bases. "I wanted to avoid another Pearl Harbor," he later explained. "I thought the Russians intended to start World War Three." The possibility of a larger war would weigh upon the minds of naval leaders in every decision they made.

In the hubbub of the emergency Joy had to make decisions and issue orders under conditions that often bypassed naval punctilio. As ship and aircraft reinforcements poured into MacArthur's theater, Joy had to decide how they would be organized. He and his staff were literally next door to MacArthur and his staff in Tokyo, and it was with them, and through them, that all naval operations had to be consolidated, negotiated, and coordinated. This could be done, was done, through face-to-face contact and word-of-mouth between their respective staffs. Consequently, there was a lessened need for message traffic between them.

Joy next had to decide how to issue orders and plans to the forces afloat, whose numbers changed daily, if not hourly, and whose composition varied from aircraft carriers to yard craft. The basics of naval operational organization were practical and time tested: fleet > task force > task group > task unit > task element. Task organizations could be created or dissolved by the stroke of a pen. Administratively the Navy was organized more regularly into carrier, battleship, and cruiser divisions, and destroyer squadrons and divisions, with equivalent organizations for the amphibious and service forces. The commanders of the administrative organizations—by rank, mostly flag officers, captains, and commanders—would be assigned command of the task organizations as they were created for operations. As Joy and his staff wrote and released operation orders to carry out what MacArthur wanted done, the forces afloat were assigned to task organizations created by the operation order.

Early on, Joy knew he could not simply place everything afloat under Struble as components of the Seventh Fleet. That is, Struble could not operate as Kinkaid had in World War II. Struble's staff was too remote from MacArthur's CINCFE headquarters and too small to manage the complexity of the unfolding developments—within the first days naval forces had to evacuate American citizens under protection of air cover, take supplies to the Republic of Korea (ROK) Army, blockade the North Korean coastline, patrol the Straits of Taiwan against a possible Chinese invasion, prepare to transport American troops to the Korean peninsula should Truman so decide, and interdict North Korean forces with naval aircraft and gunfire. (When Truman ordered the Navy to attack targets in North Korea with carrier aircraft, he effectively refuted Bradley's congressional testimony the previous October. Ironically, Bradley had testified "that he did not believe in using carrier aviation assets to attack land targets. Such a capability might be 'nice to have,' but it would not make a particularly important contribution in the initial stages of a war.")

In the hubbub of the emergency Joy had to make decisions and issue orders under conditions that often bypassed naval punctilio.

Before the war began on 25 June, Joy and Struble had had little interaction. Struble had reported to Radford in Pearl Harbor and had operated independently of MacArthur and Joy. Moreover, Joy may have heard the rumors from Washington that Struble was disliked and distrusted by some, and that Radford had a poor opinion of him. Joy's initial operation orders designated the task organization and composition for the Seventh Fleet, a move Struble would have considered a usurpation of his command, seniority, and prerogatives. Sherman corrected Joy promptly by personal message, each word carefully and tactfully chosen.

> Because the President has designated the "Seventh Fleet" to accomplish certain missions, out of consideration for a senior officer [Struble], and for reasons of naval prestige desire in drafting orders and in reports you designate as "Seventh Fleet" such forces as are under Struble's operational control and leave to him the designation of component naval task forces.

Translation: "Don't tell Struble how to run Seventh Fleet, as it might well be interpreted that the Navy lacks confidence in his ability as a fleet commander. Tell him what to do, but not how to do it."

Under no circumstances, in Sherman's estimation, could anyone question Struble's prestige as ranking naval officer in the Far East, for he had represented the Navy when Johnson and Bradley had recently visited the Philippines, and he would shortly represent the Navy in critical negotiations with Chinese Nationalist leader Chiang Kai-shek about defensive arrangements for Taiwan. In the following months, especially at Inchon, Struble would ensure that he was the naval officer most often seen in photographs with MacArthur, and that the public saw him as running naval operations in Korea. Flying his flag at sea and sporting the colorful nickname "Rip," he wanted the American public to perceive him as the Navy's counterpoint to MacArthur. Joy would operate in near obscurity in Tokyo.

USN 653242

Two SCAJAP (Supreme Commander Allies, Japan) LSTs unload critical supplies at Pohang-dong where naval forces landed the Army's 1st Cavalry Division in July 1950.

◆ ◆ ◆

The other major commander at sea reporting to Joy was Doyle, so fortuitously on hand when the shooting started. It was self-evident that he would engage in amphibious operations from the moment that Truman committed American troops to the peninsula. Nearly every soldier sent to Korea from Japan, together with 99 percent of the logistical support, would go by sea. Doyle would get them there in his capacity as Commander Attack Force (CTF 90), operating at arm's length from Seventh Fleet. Without question, Doyle would command the specialized amphibious ships once an amphibious operation began, but concurrent command of the fast carriers and their escorts, as well as the warships providing naval gunfire support, was another matter. Joy had many issues to resolve.

Foremost was the fact that an amphibious assault was one of the most risky operations in war. Doctrine learned during World War II mandated that the attacking force take control of the sea and air before the landing began, so that no enemy ships or aircraft attacked the vulnerable amphibious ships and the troops exposed in landing craft and on the beaches. In the past war, the fast carriers had taken control of the sea and the air by attacking enemy ships and aircraft at their bases or en route to the landing area. Naval aviators in command of the fast carrier task forces preferred to steam unhampered, perhaps hundreds of miles from the landing area, to seize the initiative and attack the threatening enemy preemptively. In contrast, amphibious commanders normally wanted the fast carriers nearby, first to clear out the landing area and then to establish a barrier against any enemy attacks that might develop. This latter approach tied the carriers to the amphibious assault area, which the aviators dreaded because it compromised the mobility of the carriers.

Hence, the doctrine for how best to use the fast carriers during an amphibious assault had never been resolved. Moreover, should carrier air be in conjunction with, or separate from, Air Force tactical operations? (Navy-Marine tactical air doctrine and Air Force tactical air doctrine were so incompatible that joint air operations were to prove unworkable.) In Korea, especially in the first six months of the war, the nature of the threat was uncertain. North Korea had a miniscule navy and a weak air force, but the Navy worried that the Russians might oppose at any time an amphibious assault with their submarines and aircraft. China, too, was a dangerous threat because Beijing could try to invade Taiwan or attack American forces throughout the Far East. The fast carriers, together with their screen of cruisers and destroyers, had to be prepared accordingly.

In the beachhead area itself naval aircraft and warships had to attack and destroy enemy defenses ashore, especially those that would resist the landing. This posed another question: Who would command and control the naval forces engaged in this critical close support? Which ships did what and when and under whose command were complex issues that had to be resolved and understood by everyone before hand?

Yet another complication was the participation of allied warships, especially those of the Royal Navy, which quickly arrived off Korea to augment the American fleet. To whom should they report? What tasks should they undertake? True, the Royal Navy and the United States Navy had been teammates first in the Atlantic and later in the Pacific during World War II, so in the summer of 1950 each was familiar to some extent with the other. Nonetheless, many details had to be worked out in the special circumstances of Korea.

Another great threat that could easily prevent an amphibious assault was enemy mines. Deployed in the waters transited by the amphibious assault shipping, they could delay, disrupt, and even defeat a landing operation. The Navy's minesweeping capability in the Pacific was very limited, but assuming more minesweepers could be made available, who would command them during an amphibious assault?

It was largely up to Joy to resolve these complex command and control issues almost overnight, so he relied upon doctrine, precedent, and his own judgment. The first test of Joy's operating policies materialized quickly. On 30 June, Truman authorized MacArthur to send troops to Korea. Joy's immediate task was to deploy the 1st Cavalry Division, then in Japan, to reinforce the disintegrating South Korean army and a few thousand soldiers of the 24th Infantry Division that had been airlifted to the peninsula. Doyle and his staff went to Joy's headquarters in Tokyo on 4 July to plan for the operation.

NH 96991

Marines atop a ridgeline along the Naktong River watch for signs of an enemy attack. The Naktong marked the outer edge of the Pusan Perimeter defended by the allies in the summer of 1950.

Unlike Joy's struggling staff, Doyle's staff contained some of the Navy's most expert amphibious planners, veterans of amphibious campaigns in the Pacific during World War II. With no more initial guidance than to land the division "somewhere in Korea," the staff went to work. At first the landing area was thought to be Inchon near Seoul on the west coast, but given the speed of advance of the NKPA the potential landing areas had to be moved to the south, a jump ahead of the North Koreans. Finally, Pohang-dong, a village on the east coast 70 miles north of Pusan, became the objective. It was chosen in the expectation the NKPA could not reach there by 18 July, the scheduled landing date. But given the fast advance of the NKPA down the peninsula, no one knew how close enemy troops would be to Pohang-dong.

Joy wanted the Seventh Fleet fast carriers to cover the landing in the event of enemy sea or air opposition, however unlikely. His request meant diverting the carriers from their immediate interdiction tasks and sending them to the waters off Pohang-dong. Trouble between Joy and Struble erupted when Struble learned that Joy had designated Doyle to command the aircraft carriers giving air cover to the landing. This move was unprecedented—not once during World War II had an amphibious commander ever given orders to a fast carrier. Struble predictably objected. The carriers should remain under his control, Struble argued. If Doyle wanted air cover, he should contact Joy who would order the carriers to give support. In other words, Struble would take orders from Joy but never from Doyle.

Sherman read Struble's objection and quickly responded in support. "I will not concur in placing carriers under command of [Doyle]," he wired to Radford, as one carrier admiral to another. "If naval command relationships cannot be worked out properly and harmoniously am prepared to consider your recommendations for changes in personalities." Radford was in Tokyo at the time, and he got the word to Joy. Struble retained control of the carriers.

Nonetheless, Joy and Doyle got what they wanted. Joy's operation order, with tacit approval of Sherman and Radford, directed Struble to provide close air support in the landing area as requested by Doyle. The latter would coordinate and control the operations of all aircraft in the objective area, and Doyle would define the objective area. Thus, while Struble would command the carriers per se, Doyle would decide when and where Struble's aircraft would be used. As it turned out the landing was unopposed. No air support was required, so the command relationship between Joy, Struble, and Doyle was not tested; however, it would be weeks later at Inchon.

Sherman and Radford continued to discuss the relationship between Joy and Struble. After a transpacific telephone conversation with Joy soon after the Pohang-dong operation, Sherman told Radford that he had considered an additional command echelon between Joy and Struble. He had rejected the idea because he did not want Struble to be subordinate to anyone junior to Joy. He was willing, however, to give Struble greater responsibilities that would allow naval aviator flag officers to take complete charge of the fast carrier forces. But for the moment Sherman was content with the status quo, and so matters remained.

Historian James A. Field later wrote about the growth and transition of Joy's staff as the war intensified:

> [A]s his responsibilities and his forces grew, further difficulty was presented by the inadequacy of his staff and of those of subordinate commands. The total strength, officer and enlisted, of the NavFE staff at the end of June was 188; by November it would have reached 1,227. But in the first weeks, before reinforcements arrived, the job had to be done with what was on hand. Rarely in the history of 20th century warfare can so many have been commanded by so few.
>
> It was not done without effort. [Joy's] Plans Section went to heel and toe watches, 12 hours on and 12 off. The Operations Officer moved in a cot and did such sleeping as he could in his office; his people found themselves working a 12-hour day, with an additional four-hour night watch four days out of five. For Communications the situation became a nightmare as high-precedence traffic skyrocketed; in the first days the load of encrypted messages went up by a factor of 15, and was further complicated by great quantities of interservice and U.S.-British dispatches.
>
> Somehow they made do. Even as anguished requests were sent off to Washington for more personnel, the round the clock efforts of those on the spot were accomplishing the reorganization and redeployment of available naval strength. To Naval Forces [Far East] had now been added the Seventh Fleet and British Commonwealth units; with these accessions Admiral Joy had gained all that would be available until reinforcements could come from afar.

Inchon

I also predict that large-scale amphibious operations, such as those in Sicily and Normandy, will never occur again. . . . I have participated in the two largest amphibious assaults ever made in history. In neither case were any marines present.

—General Omar N. Bradley testimony before Congress, October 1949

MACARTHUR KNEW from the first shot fired by his troops on the Korean peninsula that, eventually, he would attack the NKPA from its rear with an amphibious assault. It was but a question of where and when, not whether. Even in the first days he had considered the immediate landing of the 1st Cavalry Division at Inchon, but the astonishing speed of the NKPA advance ended such thoughts. Within weeks the NKPA had forced the embattled Americans and the ROK Army into what became known as the Pusan Perimeter. MacArthur knew he could not possibly win the war if the battlefield was confined to the Pusan area. He needed to widen the scope of UN operations.

The geographical characteristics of the Korean peninsula, as with any peninsula, begged for an amphibious assault behind enemy lines, the quintessential turning of the enemy's flank through sea power. As the NKPA had neither naval nor air forces left to protect its flanks and rear, its north-south lines of communication lay vulnerable and exposed to interdiction by naval guns, aircraft, and commando raids, and ultimately to an amphibious ground force slashing inland from a beachhead behind the enemy front. Deprived of supplies and reinforcements, the NKPA would be doomed.

As the United Nations army fought to survive during July and August, MacArthur saw not impending disaster, as did many in high places, but opportunity. The NKPA was exhausting its combat power at Pusan, and its flow of supplies over primitive roads was diminishing because of distance and naval and air interdiction. Banking that the Eighth Army could hold the perimeter, MacArthur reckoned that the time was near to counterattack with a massive amphibious assault. Getting it approved would be difficult. The JCS and the civilian leaders feared that Communist China was about to invade Taiwan and were concerned that Russia might be preparing to roll into Western Europe. Thus a third world war seemed imminent; and Korea, a diversion. Washington leaders were apprehensive and reluctant to take risks.

Then there was the matter of amphibious operations as a matter of principle. MacArthur, unlike some of his Army colleagues, believed in the utility of amphibious warfare. He had learned the art in the Pacific during World War II, from scratch operations in New Guinea to immense campaigns in the Philippines. In contrast, Bradley had publicly pronounced them obsolete, and the Air Force could hardly be expected to endorse what it had denounced as a matter of policy. And would Truman authorize the Marines to mobilize and lead an assault in light of his public excoriation of the Marines as an institution? If MacArthur prevailed, quantities of crow would be eaten in Washington.

The Navy as a matter of self-interest would of course have to support MacArthur *in principle*, but the details were another matter. Doyle first learned about Inchon in mid-July when MacArthur told him he wanted Doyle to land the 1st Cavalry Division there, even as the North Koreans were pushing the United Nations forces to the south. "I was 'slightly' upset," Doyle later said. "In fact I prayed, because the 1st Cavalry Division had no amphibious training whatsoever, and I had no ships to take them with. After the 1st Cavalry Division got to Pohang-dong . . . Inchon was moved again to the front burner."

Doyle and his staff began planning for the assault even though JCS approval was uncertain. When the Chiefs realized that Inchon violated every criterion for an amphibious assault area, they became apprehensive. The greatest incentive to press on was that, despite the risks, a landing there could reap considerable benefits. What MacArthur wanted MacArthur ultimately would get.

Doyle was glad when Major General Oliver P. "O. P." Smith, who would command the 1st Marine Division landing force, arrived on 22 August, three weeks before the tentative landing date of 15 September. Doyle had gotten to the point where he needed the troop commander's input to make the joint planning "fit together." After Smith met MacArthur that afternoon and listened to his pep talk, the Marine general, according to Doyle, "was no happier over the proposed landing area than I was."

The 15th of September had been chosen because it was the one day in the month when the tides would be optimum. "Twenty-four days remained," Smith later wrote, "in which to draw up plans, issue orders, reload the [1st Marine Division] in amphibious shipping at Kobe, forward to Korea the additional personnel and equipment to bring the 1st Provisional Marine Brigade up to strength; and then proceed to Inchon, rendezvousing with the units of the Brigade en route. On August 22nd the main body of the division was still at sea"

Smith's anxiety intensified when he met Major General Edward M. Almond, MacArthur's chief of staff, who had been double-hatted as the commander of the combined landing force of Marine and Army troops, designated X Corps. (In this first meeting, Almond condescendingly addressed Smith as "son" although they were nearly the same age.) Almond and the Army planners had no amphibious experience and hence could not conceive the difficulties involved in getting ashore at Inchon against enemy opposition. "Almond considered an amphibious landing as a purely mechanical operation," Doyle later said, "which it might be if only the

NA 80-G-422487

On 21 August 1950 Admiral Radford and General MacArthur—both commanders in chief in their own right—wait to greet Admiral Sherman and General J. Lawton Collins who were sent to Tokyo on behalf of the JCS to find out what MacArthur had in mind for operations in Korea.

Truman and the Marines

NA 127-N-A407260

President Harry S. Truman and General Clifton B. Gates, Commandant of the Marine Corps, enjoy an event at the Quantico, Virginia Marine base. Truman would anger Marine Corps leaders later in 1950 with an imprudent reference to the Marines as the "Navy's police force."

IN AUGUST 1950, AS THE North Korean People's Army steadily drove south, the 1st Provisional Marine Brigade kept the American line from disintegrating. Early one morning President Harry S. Truman wrote a private letter to Congressman Gordon McDonough, a friend of long standing, who had recommended that the Commandant of the Marine Corps be made a member of the Joint Chiefs of Staff. Truman impulsively expressed his feelings toward the Marine Corps, a service he had criticized to varying extent over the years.

It was, he wrote, "the Navy's police force" with a "propaganda machine that is almost equal to Stalin's." For unknown motives the congressman released the letter to the press, and it was published in the 18 September issue of *Time* magazine, coincidentally with the Marine's victorious amphibious assault at Inchon.

The subsequent uproar rocked the White House with a deluge of phone calls, telegrams, and letters. Truman summoned his naval aide Rear Admiral Robert L. Dennison and his press secretary Charlie Ross and told them to do something "to get me out of this." Dennison recommended that Truman write a letter of apology to General Clifton B. Cates, Commandant of the Marine Corps, and ask him to publish it.

"The President of the United State can't apologize," Ross objected.

"I don't see why not," said Dennison, "if he's made a mistake, and I assume he has."

Truman agreed with Dennison and told him to draft the letter. Dennison phoned Cates and asked him to come to the White House to help with the letter. "Hell no," replied Cates. Dennison wrote the draft alone, Truman added his own twist, and it was quickly typed and signed.

"Wasn't I invited to some Marine Corps reunion here?" the President asked.

Dennison said he had been and regrets had been sent to the Marine Corps League.

"Well, I've decided to go," said Truman. The reunion was to be held the next morning. The Secret Service worried about his security in light of the passions of the attendees, but Truman was adamant. "Ask Cates to meet me here and go with me," said Truman.

The next morning Cates waited outside while Truman met with his advisors in conference. Truman emerged accompanied by General Bradley.

"General Cates," said Truman, "we have decided I shouldn't go before the Marine Corps League." An awkward silence followed. Truman spoke again. "Well? What do you think about that? Are Marines afraid to speak up?"

"You never asked me," Cates replied.

"Well," Truman persisted. "What *do* you think?"

"I haven't told a soul about this, Mr. President," said Cates. "But I know that the Secret Service are already down there at the Statler, and the Marine Corps League must realize that you at least had the idea of going down to see them. Now, if you don't come, they'll think you are afraid to face them."

Truman banged his fist on a desk and said, "God damn it! I'll go!"

"Bradley's face was a study," Cates later said, for Bradley had attempted to dissuade President Truman from appearing.

Cates went on stage to great applause. When the audience became quiet, he said calmly, "Gentlemen, the President of the United States." The audience of Marine veterans was stunned and silent. Suddenly they erupted with cheers. "He gave a very simple but sincere talk," Dennison later said. "People were crying. A retired general on the platform removed a medal from his breast and pinned it on the President."

"You couldn't help liking Truman," said Cates long afterward, "even though he felt the way he did about the Marine Corps. Later he and I were talking over a glass of bourbon, and I told him he was absolutely right: the Marine Corps did have a 'propaganda machine.' But we were fighting for our lives. What else would *you* do? Truman just grinned."

The two luckiest things that happened to the Marine Corps during his watch, said Cates, were the outbreak of war in Korea and the Truman letter. Cates observed: "They saved the Marine Corps."

NA 80-G-422492

MacArthur takes Sherman and Collins in tow for his forthcoming Inchon "performance." The JCS concurred in the attack on Inchon, in large measure because Sherman told his colleagues it could be done; or, as Doyle had said, it "was not impossible."

enemy would play dead. He was inclined to be arrogant and dictatorial and often confused himself with his boss." The Army planners thus considered the Inchon landing a fait accompli and concentrated on what would come later, the seizure of Seoul and the destruction of the NKPA.

Doyle was concerned that Almond and the Army staff were shielding MacArthur from the details of the planning and that MacArthur might not be aware of the risks. Almond, however, barred Doyle from MacArthur's door. "The General is not interested in details," Almond told Doyle.

"The General is making the decision," Doyle responded. "He must know what that decision involves, and I intend to see that he does so."

The opportunity to brief MacArthur came on 23 August when Sherman and General J. Lawton Collins, the Army chief of staff, arrived in Tokyo to consult with MacArthur on Inchon. As Collins later testified, he and Sherman had gone there "to find out exactly what the plans were. Frankly, we were somewhat in the dark, and as it was a matter of great concern, we went out to discuss it with General MacArthur."

Doyle and his staff were ready. In the inevitable discussion over the length and intensity of the prelanding bombardment, Doyle's gunnery officer illuminated the dangers by telling his audience that enemy shore batteries dominated the shipping channel and had to be eliminated. If all the emplacements in the reconnaissance photographs had guns and crews, he said, based on World War II experience it would take from four to five days to take them out. MacArthur commented that that length of time would take away the advantage of surprise and reveal allied intentions.

Sherman impulsively interrupted. "One or two days would be enough," he said. "I wouldn't hesitate to take a ship up off Wolmi-do after a day of bombardment."

"Spoken like a Farragut," MacArthur responded warmly.

Doyle was inwardly furious, for Sherman was a naval aviator, and Doyle felt he knew little, if anything, about amphibious operations. "Sherman was like the boxer's manager," Doyle later said, "who sends his tiger into the ring with the comforting words, 'Go in there, boy. He can't hurt us.' Admiral Sherman's remark was gratuitous, which I bitterly resented. We were never mutual admirers. However I held my tongue, and when I cooled off five or ten years later I called the episode the 'John Wayne Exchange.'"

As the briefing neared its end, Doyle spoke directly to MacArthur. No one had asked his opinion, said Doyle, but if he were asked his best answer was that Inchon "is not impossible."

"If we find we cannot make it," responded MacArthur, "we will withdraw."

"No General," said Doyle. "We don't know how to do that. Once we start ashore we keep going." ("Now that may sound a bit 'John Wayne-ish' too," Doyle later admitted, "but the thought of our failure in an amphibious operation had never entered my mind, and it didn't then.")

In a lecture at the Naval War College in 1974, Doyle recalled MacArthur's closing pitch:

> MacArthur then began speaking, and he was superb. He gave his reasons for preferring Inchon to Posung-myon/Kunsan. Inchon was the closest point to

Seoul, it cut the enemy's lines of communication to the south, and it had the element of surprise. The enemy would not believe that we would select Inchon, with all its hazards, as a spot to land. He compared Inchon to Wolfe's surprise landing and the capture of Quebec. He also said that a landing at Inchon was a 10,000-to-one shot and that for a five dollar bet he would win fifty thousand: he saw that Inchon and the capture of Seoul would end the war. He concluded with, "We shall land at Inchon and I shall crush them!" Now John Wayne couldn't top that, I'm sure. I have said of General MacArthur, many times, that if he had gone on the stage no one would have heard of his contemporary, another actor, John Barrymore.

Sherman was still worried about the hydrographic hazards and remained skeptical, despite his exclamation during Doyle's presentation. The next day, 24 August, Sherman spent better than an hour with MacArthur. When he emerged, Sherman had been convinced. "I wish I had that man's confidence," Sherman remarked to Joy.

Radford felt that the Navy and Marine Corps supported MacArthur and that the greatest opposition came from within the general's own staff. On a later trip to Tokyo Radford attended a somber planning conference and listened to a staff officer deliver an especially pessimistic assessment of the risks in a contemplated operation. "General," said MacArthur when it ended, "there is just one thing you've forgotten."

"What's that, General MacArthur?" the planner replied.

"My luck," said MacArthur.

Sherman and Collins returned to Washington to consult with the full JCS and Secretary Johnson, and the JCS approved Inchon on 29 August. MacArthur gave credit to Sherman for getting Washington's approval.

◆◆◆

When Sherman returned to Washington, he summoned Arleigh Burke into his office and told him about conditions in Tokyo. The Inchon invasion was going to be touch and go, said Sherman, and Radford had convinced the CNO that Joy 's staff was not prepared to plan and coordinate wartime operations. Joy's chief of staff was Rear Admiral Albert K. Morehouse, a naval aviator a year senior to Burke. Although Morehouse had commanded an escort carrier in the last months of the war, he was without wartime staff experience, and as an aviator, he was unfamiliar with amphibious operations. Hence, Joy desperately needed a staff flag officer with combat and staff experience to organize and direct its wartime responsibilities, especially for the immediate needs of Inchon.

Courtesy U.S. Naval Institute

Rear Admiral Arleigh A. Burke, a future Chief of Naval Operations, joined the Naval Forces, Far East staff just before Inchon. Sherman wanted Burke to report on developments by a separate and privileged communications system, but Burke insisted that Joy see everything that he sent to or received from Washington.

Burke was exactly the person Joy needed, for not only had he been a renowned wartime destroyer commander in the South Pacific, he had also become famous as chief of staff to Marc Mitscher.

Having explained what Joy needed and why, Sherman asked Burke if he would go to Tokyo as Joy's deputy chief of staff, with the most immediate priority of directing the staff for the forthcoming Inchon assault. "Sherman still had misgivings," Burke later said. Sherman expressed his concern that Burke might be miffed that the billet would be of lesser stature than what he had held with Mitscher. Burke said he had no such reservations and would take the job, perhaps realizing he would be getting out of Washington and ridding whatever stigma remained from his role in the "revolt of the admirals." Burke's only immediate worry was that Joy's staff might resent his intrusion as the "expert" from Washington coming in to tell them how to run their business.

Sherman said it was possible but assumed Burke would quickly be welcomed. Sherman then introduced an additional role for Burke: to be his eyes and ears to apprise Sherman of unfolding developments through a super Blue Flag channel restricted solely to Sherman and Burke. For this purpose, he gave Burke a special set of encryption rotors. It was a preposterous idea for any number of reasons, the least of which was that Burke probably never had used a coding machine or the rotors that went with it. Finding a communications specialist surreptitiously to decrypt and encrypt messages for him would raise suspicions within the staff. Then there was the moral issue: would it be ethical for Burke to communicate directly with Sherman without Joy's knowledge?

Burke was in a bind, which he cleverly resolved. Anything he proposed to send to Sherman, said Burke, had to be shown first to Joy. Anything he got from Sherman he would also show to Joy. Sherman had to agree. As far as we know, not a single eyes-only message ever passed between Sherman and Burke. While Burke routinely drafted and often released Blue Flag messages to Sherman, they were always in Joy's name and had Joy's explicit or implicit approval.

> The upshot was that Burke proved invaluable to Joy through the crises of the last four months of 1950.

As if Burke needed any incentive to go to Korea, Sherman gratuitously promised Burke any rear admiral's job he wanted once things were under control in Joy's bailiwick, perhaps within three or four months. Burke did not take the promise seriously, for even a CNO could neither predict nor control the conditions that influenced flag officer assignments. The upshot was that Burke proved invaluable to Joy through the crises of the last four months of 1950.

Joy summarized to Sherman and Radford in late January 1951 what Burke meant to him:

> Burke is my daily contact with top echelons GHQ where his influence is healthy for Navy. He is also staff coordinator for joint and combined operations as well as deputy chief of staff. Consider essential that flag officer with broad knowledge naval operations and experience in the service relationships fill this role. My 2 flag officers [Burke and Morehouse] cover contacts with 5 generals of Air Force and about 10 of Army on matters on which rank of conferees is important.

After periodic exchanges of messages between Sherman, Radford, and Joy, Burke finally got command of a cruiser division in May 1951. It would be a short tour, for he rejoined Joy in July as a member of the UN negotiating team for the fruitless armistice talks.

◆ ◆ ◆

Doyle and Smith were still unhappy with the choice of Inchon, but while MacArthur orated and twisted arms and the JCS thought about it, their superb staffs pressed on with the planning. Within three days of Smith's arrival, they had completed a detailed plan for Inchon, and two days later they issued a preliminary operation order. Years later Doyle commented on the risks as he saw them at the time. "It has always been my conviction," he wrote, "that, given the enemy forces, an amphibious landing can be made anywhere if the commander is willing to accept the risk of the [estimated] losses. Naturally the commander would prefer the landing in a place where the losses could be minimized—which is all O. P. Smith and I were talking about."

Still to be determined was the command structure for the landing. Doyle would have preferred being in complete command at Inchon as he had been at Pohang-dong, where he had been responsible for planning and executing the landing of the 1st Cavalry Division. Struble, a fleet commander and senior to him by a full rank, had been left out of that operation; his sole task had been to provide carrier air support when and if Doyle asked for it, a role that in effect made him subordinate to Doyle. It would be different at Inchon: Struble intended to be in command with Doyle as his subordinate.

Indeed, in July Sherman, Radford, and Joy had discussed command relationships by phone and Blue Flag messages. While Joy had consistently advocated Doyle's position, Sherman refused to make Struble subordinate to anyone but Joy. More to the point, Sherman wanted Struble to have greater responsibilities under Joy and to delegate Seventh Fleet carrier operations to aviation flag officers. Hence, Joy had no choice but to appoint Struble the naval commander for Inchon.

On 25 August, presumably after conferring with Sherman during his visit to Tokyo, Joy informally told Struble he would command the Inchon operation. Joy made the assignment official when he issued his operation order and at Struble's suggestion designated him Commander Joint Task Force 7. The "joint" designation was intentional, for it gave Struble command and control over all the services in the landing. Thus, Almond would not take command of X Corps until he had established his command post ashore, in accordance with standard amphibious doctrine.

Courtesy U.S. Air Force

Lieutenant General George E. Stratemeyer (left), commander of the Far East Air Forces, converses with General Earle E. Partridge, commander of the Fifth Air Force. The Air Force wanted to control all aircraft, including Navy and Marine planes, operating in Korea. Admirals Sherman, Radford, and Joy, with MacArthur's support, successfully resisted the Air Force effort.

Neither of Struble's immediate subordinates, Doyle and Smith, was pleased at the prospect of working with him. When Smith had been Assistant Commandant of the Marine Corps, he had been assigned to work with the Navy establishing doctrine for command relationships in amphibious operations. The naval representative was Rear Admiral Jerauld Wright, who later became Commander in Chief, Atlantic Fleet. He and Smith got along well and were nearing agreement. Unexpectedly Struble intervened in their discussions. "He put us back where we started," Smith later wrote. "About a year later he was overruled, and the present [1956] doctrine of command relationships, almost identical with what Admiral Wright and I had agreed upon, was adopted and published."

◆◆◆

Struble used his authority directly by not allowing the Air Force to participate at Inchon. "Like most naval commanders," Struble later wrote, "[I] was wary of the elaborate coordinating arrangements which always seemed necessary when Air Force units took part in invasions. As a veteran of Normandy [I] could well remember that despite all of the Air Force units present in England before the invasion, that the Air Force was

Naval commanders gather on board a Seventh Fleet ship off Korea to discuss upcoming air operations in support of the Inchon landing: Left to right, Rear Admiral Edward C. Ewen, Commander Carrier Division 1, the Fast Carrier Force (Task Force 77); Vice Admiral Arthur D. Struble, Commander Seventh Fleet; and Rear Admiral John M. Hoskins, Commander Carrier Division 3.

unable to support the amphibious landing properly, and their efforts in this respect were practically nil." As Commander Seventh Fleet during interdiction operations, he had discovered that Air Force procedures were still cumbersome, if not unworkable. Knowing that having Navy, Marine, and Air Force planes in the same air space over Inchon would complicate coordination and control, Struble simply made Inchon a no-fly zone for the Air Force.

The Air Force was infuriated at its exclusion, as it wanted operational control over all aircraft flying over the Korean landmass, including carrier planes. More specifically, Lieutenant General George E. Stratemeyer, commanding the Far East Air Forces (Joy's opposite number), wanted to control all aircraft operating from Korean and Japanese airfields, including Marine air and Navy ASW patrol and transport aircraft. Stratemeyer persisted in this demand well after Inchon, which Sherman, Radford, and Joy unreservedly opposed as yet another effort to unify the services, which had been a major feature of the "revolt of the admirals."

By late December Stratemeyer had gotten his proposal included in a comprehensive operation plan prepared for MacArthur's signature. MacArthur sent the plan to Joy for his review, and Joy told Sherman and Radford what he thought of it. It was an example, he said, of the continuing effort to make the Navy an auxiliary service. Sherman immediately responded. "You may quote me," he told Joy and Radford, "as having said that I will not accept any formula that puts naval aircraft under Air Force control merely because they are land based."

Radford had the last word. "As CNO states," he told Joy, "he will not accept any formula that puts naval aircraft under Air Force control just because they are land based. That particular question is settled. . . . It seems unfortunate but true that you have a continuing selling job to do where [MacArthur] is concerned and one which you have successfully accomplished so far. Good luck in your present efforts."

◆◆◆

Sherman had returned to Washington, and JCS approval for Inchon while likely was still open. "Until that decision was received in Tokyo," Struble later wrote, "any planning had a preliminary and uncertain status about it." When JCS approval (albeit restrained) was received on 29 August, the invasion was on. Once assigned command of the Inchon assault, Struble stayed in Tokyo with a small staff and interjected himself into the planning already underway with Doyle, Smith, and their staffs. Most of their plans he approved, others he modified after discussion. Once he, Doyle, and Smith achieved an understanding, Struble got entree to MacArthur and informed him of the overall plan. (No CINCFE staff officer, even Almond, would refuse the imperious Struble admission to the inner sanctum!) "I told him what we were going to do," Struble later wrote. "I did not ask for any decisions." Struble issued his operation order two weeks before the landing, largely incorporating the

NA 80-G-423190

Major General Oliver P. Smith, Commanding General, 1st Marine Division, and Rear Admiral James H. Doyle, Commander Task Force 90, the Attack Force, confer on board the admiral's flagship Mount McKinley *(AGC 7) just before the Inchon invasion.*

detailed planning of the Doyle-Smith staffs. Operation orders from MacArthur and Joy authenticated Struble's order. The invasion force continued its preparations for Inchon.

The plans had assumed that the 1st Provisional Marine Brigade, then engaging the NKPA on the Pusan Perimeter, would be pulled out of line on or about 1 September and would rejoin its parent command, the 1st Marine Division, en route to Korea. Lieutenant General Walton H. Walker, commanding the Eighth Army tenuously holding the perimeter, at first assented. But as the Marines began withdrawing, the NKPA broke through, so alarming Walker that he changed his mind and refused to release the brigade. The brigade had saved the perimeter, Radford later said, so it is understandable that Walker was reluctant to see it leave. Walker's apprehension was also predictable. When Radford, Sherman, and Collins had taken lunch with Walker at his headquarters near Taegu on 22 August, the headquarters had been set up to retreat on an hour's notice in the event the Communists broke through.

Almond was willing to leave the Marines with Walker and—presumably with MacArthur's approval—intended to substitute the 32d Infantry Regiment to land at Inchon in the brigade's place. Such a change was preposterous. Smith and Doyle met with Joy on 2 September to express their dismay and seek resolution. The landing, they said, would be touch and go in any event. The experienced

NA 809-G-423206

An LST quietly slips into Inchon harbor in the early hours of 15 September before the landings. Admiral Doyle designated eight of these ships, loaded with ammunition, vehicles, and supplies, for direct beaching on the heels of the Marines' Red Beach assault. Thirty-nine other LSTs pressed into Korean War service also delivered the much-needed supplies essential to the successes ashore at Inchon.

Doyle's Army Passengers

THE INCHON TASK FORCE slogged up the west coast of Korea, and Vice Admiral C. Turner Joy sent a final sitrep to CNO Forrest P. Sherman and Commander in Chief, Pacific Arthur W. Radford on D-Day-2: "General MacArthur and large staff now aboard *Mt. McKinley* in Sasebo after many changes prospective plans and dodging typhoon. Doyle has his hands full with all that staff and fighting a war too. Typhoon has probably made many Marines and soldiers appreciate the rigors of seagoing life but has had no other serious effect to date."

Doyle later recalled:

> [We] were rolling handsomely. After thirty minutes of that the order came from General MacArthur to the effect, "Couldn't the course be changed to eliminate the rolling?" It could be and I sent word to the captain. . . . He changed course just enough to ease the rolling, but, knowing that he had an appointment at Inchon, the captain soon came back to the uncomfortable course. Another message, another change, and finally we were in the lee of Korea. [The typhoon] was proceeding up the east coast and course was resumed for Inchon. It's helpful to be lucky.
>
> Breakfast the following morning was served in [the captain's] cabin. As was customary, my seat was at the head of the table, and I pointedly indicated a seat to my right when General MacArthur entered the cabin. Just as pointedly he ignored the seat and took a seat at the far end of the table. An amusing thought came to my mind from an old story, and the punch line was, "Where Murphy sits is the head of the table." I didn't share my amusement.

Once the landing was under way, X Corps commander Major General Edward M. Almond, embarked in *Mount McKinley*, asked Doyle to expedite the unloading of his communications van, so that it would be in place when he established his headquarters ashore and took command of the troops.

After Almond's inquiry, Doyle later wrote in a letter to Colonel Robert Heinl:

> I asked the captain of the AKA [amphibious transport], which had the van, for the dope. The van was in fact Almond's living quarters and was loaded below the combat equipment. I informed the captain to let me know if further inquiry was made, and that I intended to tell Almond we'd cut a hole in the bottom of the ship to get it out. Apparently Almond did not follow up on the first inquiry.
>
> Several days later, Almond invited me ashore for dinner, and of course we spent the time over drinks before and after dinner in the van. It was a beautifully built and appointed small-size house trailer. Sturdier of course than those you'll meet on the highway. It had two couches which converted into beds . . . a head and a shower, ice box, desk, and a telephone which I suppose made it a communications van.
>
> It was my first look and I thought that war is not so tough for some soldiers. I contrasted that later at Hungnam when [Marine Major General] Field Harris would come out to the ship for a hair cut and a bath.

NA 80-G-423189

Rear Admiral James H. Doyle, Commander Task Force 90 and the Navy's premier amphibious expert, pauses on the flag bridge of Mount McKinley *on the way to Inchon. Doyle had personally briefed his ship captains as to the vagaries of the landing sites and what he expected of the officers.*

SC 348448

Having watched the first wave of assaults on Wolmi-do, General MacArthur takes time to relax on the flag bridge of Mount McKinley *(AGC 7) with his senior advisors, left to right, Rear Admiral Doyle, Brigadier General Edwin K. Wright, and Major General Edward M. Almond.*

Marine brigade was essential to its success; the Army regiment had neither the training nor the experience for such a dangerous amphibious landing. Moreover, the Marines had been in combat; the soldiers of the 32d had not been in action. It was madness to substitute raw soldiers for veteran Marines. Joy agreed and arranged a meeting with the Army commanders. Only two weeks remained before D-Day.

Joy, Struble, Doyle, and Smith entered Almond's office the next day to confront Army generals Almond, Clark L. Ruffner, and Edwin K. Wright. Almond's attitude was that there was nothing to discuss. He confirmed his decision that the Marine brigade would remain at Pusan and that the 32d Infantry would take its place in the first wave at Inchon. Joy expressed his objections and became infuriated that Almond had so little understanding of amphibious warfare and the dangerous consequences of excluding the Marine brigade. Hot words flared between Almond and Joy while the others watched the fireworks. Finally, Joy paused, turned to Smith, and asked for his opinion.

Smith explained the danger of last-minute substitutions. If the 32d Infantry was forced upon him, he would not allow its soldiers to land in the first wave because it could not do what the Marine brigade could do. In effect, explained Smith, Almond was proposing to reduce unacceptably the combat power of the landing force to the point where the risk of failure would be unacceptable.

Almond was unmovable. "General Headquarters" would take that risk, he said. General MacArthur would be on Doyle's flagship and would take the responsibility for calling off the landing if necessary. Almond's inability to comprehend the impossibility of withdrawing once the landing was underway appalled the naval commanders.

Struble proposed a compromise: Use the Marine brigade at Inchon as planned, and station a regiment from the 7th Infantry Division as a floating reserve for General Walker at Pusan. Almond agreed to think about it, and the meeting ended. An hour later the commander of the Marine brigade phoned Smith and said the brigade would be released to land at Inchon.

Joy was still worried that MacArthur might change his mind at the last minute and said so in a Blue Flag to Sherman and Radford summarizing the meeting. "Made strong representations," he reported,

> that without this brigade the success of the operation would be jeopardized beyond reasonable risk. Other units untrained in amphibious operations suggested by [MacArthur] staff to substitute for brigade in landing not considered acceptable substitutes by us. . . . Situation now clarified but lack of understanding of need for trained assault troops for amphibious operations plus Marine's demonstrated superior ability to prevent enemy advances has resulted in unwillingness of [Walker] to release brigade and reluctance of [MacArthur] to order it released. A new serious enemy breakthrough may cause Marines to be ordered not to withdraw. Believe [MacArthur] would continue forthcoming operation even without brigade. Will advise developments.

NA 90-G-423215

LCVPs from Union *(AKA 106) circle in the transport area before approaching the line of departure off Inchon on the first day of the landings, 15 September. Succeeding waves of Navy LCVPs carried Marines to the assault beaches at Inchon.*

Radford replied in support: "Concur wholly with position you have taken regarding utter necessity inclusion of First Marine Brigade as part of assault force. Further consider that you are entirely justified is expressing view that without brigade the force will be deficient in qualified amphibious troops to a degree which renders operation as a whole unjustifiably hazardous."

Joy and Struble finally were able to confirm that the Marines would land in full strength. "The operation has a good chance of success," Joy reported a week before the landing. "The great benefits accruing if operation successful warrant the great calculated risks involved. . . . Joy says go ahead—and pray."

Struble had much the same assessment a day later: "Consider that military, political and psychological advantages accruing if total operation successful warrants acceptance risks involved."

◆ ◆ ◆

The Inchon landing was indeed successful, and afterward in his action report Smith expressed his reasons why it went well:

> Under the circumstances . . . it is my conviction that the successful assault of Inchon could have been accomplished only by United States Marines. This conviction, I am certain, is shared by everyone who planned, executed, or witnessed the assault. My statement is not to be construed as a comparison of the fighting qualities of the various units of the Armed Forces. It simply means that because of their many years of specialized training in amphibious warfare, in conjunction with the Navy, only the United States Marines had the requisite "know-how" to formulate the plans within the limited time available and to execute those plans flawlessly without additional training or rehearsal.
>
> To put it another way, I know that if any other unit or our Armed Forces had been designated as the Landing Force for the assault on Inchon, that unit would have required many, many months of specialized training, including joint training with the Navy, which is a regular part of the Marines everyday life.

USA SC 348522

Top military commanders at Inchon join MacArthur (front seat) for his tour of the port and visits to command posts: Rear seat, right to left, Admiral Struble, General Smith, and General Almond.

Maggie Higgins at Inchon

WE STILL WONDER today why the Inchon invasion surprised the North Koreans, for the imminent assault was common knowledge. Some 86 correspondents, representing six countries, knew about it. They occupied some 19 ships in the amphibious task force, and a platoon of public affairs officers, as Robert Heinl later wrote in *Victory at High Tide* (1979), were dispatched to "serve and yet curb this mettlesome crew."

On the day after the Inchon landing, correspondent Marguerite "Maggie" Higgins of the *New York Herald Tribune* asked to see Rear Admiral James H. Doyle, Commander Amphibious Group 1. The admiral had already heard of her. By tenaciously overcoming sexist obstacles she had landed with the fifth wave on D-Day, had seen combat up close, and was becoming legendary for her extraordinary bravery and toughness. That morning she had gone ashore with General Douglas MacArthur and had returned to Doyle's flagship *Mount McKinley* (AGC 7) to file her story. "Naturally I agreed to see her," Doyle later recalled, "and she was brought to my cabin. Miss Higgins was tall and slender, she was dressed in a coverall, and her short, light brown hair was tousled and in ringlets. She had a smudge of dirt on her cheek. She was beautiful."

Higgins told Doyle she wished to remain overnight in *Mount McKinley*. Doyle, an officer and gentleman of the old school, had a problem. Vice Admiral C. Turner Joy, Commander Naval Forces, Far East, had decreed that women correspondents had to be billeted in the hospital ship. Not only was Doyle bound by this order, but there was no room on his flagship because MacArthur and his staff, as well as the Marine staffs, were living on board. Thus if she remained overnight, explained Doyle, it would deprive four officers of their room, and in addition it would tie up a head for her exclusive use.

Higgins dismissed Doyle's objections. She wanted to be treated the same as the male correspondents. If they could remain overnight, so could she, and that meant sleeping on the flagship. "Furthermore," she declared, "you'd be surprised how long I can go without using the head."

Doyle was momentarily flustered. "Interesting," he mumbled. He recovered his poise. "Nevertheless, you must go to the hospital ship tonight."

Weather intervened preventing any boat traffic the remainder of the night. Doyle was stuck with Maggie Higgins. "I sent for the bull surgeon," Doyle later recalled, "and learned that he could give Marguerite a cot in the dispensary and move the corpsman now occupying the space. So that crisis was solved. I was grateful that it made my inevitable defeat acceptable."

Doyle later met Higgins in Tokyo: "We had a pleasant visit and a few drinks at the former Imperial Hotel—a fond memory. She wrote well, and she had magnificent courage. Months later back in the states, one of my attention callers called my attention to an article in the *Ladies' Home Journal* which she had written. She had included a paragraph referring to the incident on the *Mount McKinley* and giving me my comeuppance but good."

NA 80-G-421944

Vice Admiral Arthur D. Stuble, Commander Seventh Fleet, and Major General Oliver P. Smith (in Marine battle dress) flank MacArthur as they come ashore at Inchon, accompanied by a gaggle of correspondents and staff. Smith's Marines were already on the road to Seoul. Correspondent Maggie Higgins is among the crowd, having intimidated Doyle into allowing her to remain on his flagship so she could see the action.

To the Yalu and Back

"Army still buoyantly hopeful war will be over by Christmas."

—Message, Vice Admiral C. Turner Joy to Washington, 26 November 1950

THE WAR SEEMED nearly over. The landing at Inchon, the recapture of Seoul, and the breakout at Pusan created a momentum that drove the NKPA out of South Korea. The Truman administration and the JCS authorized MacArthur to cross the 38th Parallel and invade North Korea. Exactly what MacArthur was expected to do there, and how he was to do it, became a contentious debate between MacArthur and Washington. Was he to advance to the Yalu—the China border—and then permanently occupy North Korea? Or was he expected to accomplish something less than that? The JCS directives were laden with qualifications and rules of engagement to reduce the risks of war with China, which would neither want MacArthur's army near its border nor North

NH 96378

Marines encounter heavy fighting in Seoul, the sprawling South Korean capital defended by more that 20,000 North Koreans. By late September, after a costly house-to-house fight, the Marines had liberated the battered city.

General MacArthur boards Missouri *(BB 63) off Inchon on 21 September 1950. The general hoped naval forces would enable him to secure all of Korea for the UN coalition by carrying out an amphibious landing at Wonsan on the peninsula's east coast.*

Korea permanently occupied by the ROK Army and its allies.

"Korea was the first war to be fought from Washington," Radford later commented. According to Radford, the JCS seemed incapable of planning or foresight. Once the Inchon invasion was a near certainty, it was obvious that American and ROK forces would have to cross the 38th Parallel to exploit the victory, and in particular to close the trap on the NKPA. Not until 27 September, 12 days after the Inchon landing, did the JCS authorize MacArthur to enter North Korea to destroy the NKPA. Radford speculated that the delay in reaching this political decision might well have retarded operations after Inchon, enabling many North Korean troops and units to escape northward up the east coast because the Americans were unable to get across their line of retreat.

Enamored with the success of Inchon, MacArthur ordered a follow-up amphibious landing at Wonsan on the eastern coast of North Korea to block the retreat of NKPA forces there. Joy and his staff thought the idea wholly unnecessary. In their judgment, the X Corps could reach Wonsan faster and easier by simply marching overland from Inchon, compared to transporting it there by sea. Joy expressed his objections to MacArthur's acting chief of staff, Major General Doyle O. Hickey, who was sympathetic but said that MacArthur had made up his mind and nothing would change it. Joy resignedly returned to his headquarters to make the necessary plans.

◆◆◆

Joy and Burke had become increasingly aware of the threat of mines, the sole means by which the North Koreans could prevent amphibious assaults along their coasts. The Soviets, who were experts in mine warfare, were providing the North Koreans with an arsenal of mines and technical assistance. The North Koreans could deploy the mines in their home waters using small craft and could easily predict the most likely beaches on which the Americans would land next. Enemy capability became intention became fact. Reconnaissance planes sighted hundreds, then thousands of mines in the waters off Wonsan, forcing Joy and Burke to think how to eliminate them. Otherwise, there could be no landing and an embarrassing admission that fishing boats had denied the United States Navy control of the sea. Joy had no intention of telling MacArthur that the Navy could not carry out his orders.

Because of postwar demobilization and institutional neglect, the Navy had but a handful of minesweepers, small ships with wooden hulls outfitted with paravanes and other special equipment. Many more would be needed for any hope of clearing the mines surrounding the approaches to Wonsan before the 20 October D-Day. Responding to an early warning from Joy, Sherman recommended that Japanese minesweepers augment the handful of American minesweepers. Having received the CNO's implicit blessing, Burke set about getting Japanese permission.

Burke knew that the Japanese government employed perhaps a hundred minesweepers in a continuing program to clear the thousands of American mines, emplaced during the war, from Japanese

NH 91430

Rear Admiral Arleigh Burke greets retired Japanese admiral Kichisaburo Nomura aboard Burke's flagship Los Angeles *(CA 135), later in the war. Normura had been ambassador to the United States when Japan attacked Pearl Harbor. Nine years later Burke sought his counsel on probable Chinese and North Korean intentions in the Far East. Having been relieved of duty on Joy's staff, Burke now commanded Cruiser Division 5. He would soon go ashore again to serve with Joy during armistice negotiations.*

waters. How was Burke to get permission and cooperation from the Japanese to send their minesweepers and expert crews (largely former officers and sailors of the defunct Imperial Japanese Navy) to Korean waters? The legal, political, and moral obstacles seemed insuperable.

Burke decided to find a way without asking permission from higher authority because from past experience the answer would be No. "If you're going to do anything quickly," Burke later said, "then you've got to do it before you get permission to do it. But you must be sure it's the right thing to do."

Wanting to learn about the culture and the thinking of his former Japanese enemies, and Asians in general, Burke had already developed a good relationship with Kichisaburo Nomura, an Americanophile who had been Japan's foreign minister and later envoy to the United States at the time of Pearl Harbor. Burke liked and respected the old retired admiral and was accustomed to asking his advice and counsel.

Conditioned in the ways of the Japanese mind by Nomura, Burke contacted Takeo Okubo, the civilian director of the Maritime Safety Agency that operated the minesweepers. Burke met Okubo when the officer briefed members of the Japanese government. Burke went to Okubo's office and laid out charts of Wonsan, incidentally revealing classified information to a Japanese civilian who was not cleared for such material, a risk that Burke took upon himself.

"This is where we are going," said Burke. "It's heavily mined, we

NA 80-G-422376

Vice Admiral Arthur Struble (left) and Rear Admiral James Doyle (right) listen as Major General Edward Almond, Commanding General, X Corps, discusses his plans for the Wonsan operation.

have only twelve minesweepers, and we need more."

Okubo understood and agreed.

"The operation has begun, troops are loading into transports, and there is no turning back, " said Burke.

Okubo understood and agreed.

"We need your minesweepers," said Burke.

Okubo again understood. Nevertheless, he explained, the Japanese constitution, imposed by MacArthur, did not allow Japan to go to war, which it would be doing if its minesweepers entered Korean waters in support of the American war effort. The problem was beyond Okubo's authority to resolve.

Burke attempted to counter Okubo's reservations. "You can do it," he insisted. The minesweepers were unarmed and would neither be committing an act of war nor harming any North Koreans. "You sweep mines," said Burke, "you get rid of mines. It's the same as having your own cargo ships there manned by civilian crews, as you do now."

"It's a greater problem than that," said Okubo. "I can't make a decision on that."

"Who can?" asked Burke.

Okubo said Japanese Prime Minister Shigoru Yoshida, whom Burke also knew from briefings. Burke said he would see Yoshida, knowing that Okubo would phone ahead saying Burke was on the way.

Burke audaciously set off to see the head of the Japanese government on a matter of the greatest delicacy, with neither the knowledge nor the permission of either MacArthur or the State Department. Had his mission backfired his career would have been over.

NA 80-G421430

Underwater demolition team members from destroyer transport Diachenko *(APD 123) pour over charts of a North Korean minefield off Wonsan. The operation to clear Wonsan would take 15 days and claim three U.S. and two allied minesweepers.*

NA 80-G-668794

Joy visits Struble on his flagship Missouri *(BB 63) on 18 October 1950 off Wonsan for talks on mine-clearing operations. Arleigh Burke, as deputy chief of staff to Joy, had worked mightily to get Japanese minesweepers into Wonsan to assist the depleted United States mine warfare forces.*

NA 80-G-422164

Sailors on board minesweeper Mockingbird *(AMS 27) deploy an acoustic hammer box to locate the magnetic-influence mines discovered during sweeping operations off Wonsan. This type of mine disrupted the final sweep of the channel, forcing postponement of the landing.*

Yoshida received Burke and politely listened to him explain the urgency of his needs. No longer a blunt warrior but a subtle diplomat, Burke did not want to compel Yoshida to say either yes or no. Burke listened carefully to the nuances and intricacies of the Japanese language translated into English, and he sensed that Yoshida was expressing his implied assent to using the minesweepers. "I wish I'd had a tape recorder then," Burke later reminisced, "and could have recorded the exact wording, because he didn't agree and he didn't disagree."

Burke hustled back to Okubo to negotiate the details with him and his deputy, Kyozo Tamura, formerly a captain in the Imperial Japanese Navy, whom Burke discovered to be brilliant, pragmatic, and undoubtedly one of the greatest minesweeping experts in the world. Both Japanese leaders cooperated enthusiastically. The three men agreed that the Japanese would assign 20 minesweepers to Wonsan and pay double wages to the crews as an incentive.

Burke had gotten what he wanted, and MacArthur approved their use. Meanwhile Sherman scraped the barrel for other resources, and the combined American-Japanese minesweeping force began clearing the approaches to Wonsan.

Struble demanded of Joy that he be given direct control of the Wonsan minesweeping operations, both in light of his experience as Pacific mine force commander at the end of World War II and in his capacity as commander of Joint Task Force 7, as he had been at Inchon. Burke would not hear of it, for he trusted neither Struble's expertise nor his sensitivity in dealing with the Japanese. Consequently, the minesweeping operations came directly under Doyle as the amphibious task force commander.

As events were to prove, the mine clearing took longer than anticipated, and three minesweepers were sunk. Even though ROK forces had captured Wonsan by land making an amphibious landing unnecessary, MacArthur would not scrub the operation. Hence, the Marines languished offshore while generals and admirals fumed and squabbled. Eventually mine-free lanes to the beach were cleared allowing the Marines to make an administrative landing on 26 October, six days after the planned D-Day.

To what extent the Japanese minesweepers were used and what they accomplished at Wonsan is not to be found in open literature. Analysis of recently released Blue Flag messages between Struble and Joy indicate that 10 were employed at Wonsan, 10 in other harbors, and that one hit a mine in Wonsan. Their presence was diplomatically sensitive, so Struble directed the senior naval officers at Wonsan to ask the press not to report their employment. Cagle and Mason did not record their activity in *The Sea War in Korea* (1957); the book's description of the operation was in large measure based upon contemporary interviews with the participants who apparently did not talk about the Japanese, or if they did Cagle and Mason chose not to record it. *United States Naval Operations—Korea* (1962) by Field simply records that eight contract Japanese sweepers were employed at Wonsan, with no further details.

◆ ◆ ◆

Burke later recalled the jubilation after Wonsan:

> People were walking on clouds and were absolutely confident that the war had been won. There was not very much discussion about the possibility of North Korea pulling up her socks and being able to attack, because it didn't seem possible for that. But there was very little discussion about the Chinese possibility, or the Soviets' possible intervention. . . . They thought this was too improbable. At the same time there was no discussion that I know of about the defense of South Korea.

As September evolved into October the Chinese government announced in various ways that it would not tolerate American troops in North Korea, yet the Americans remained skeptical. Burke went to his principal counselor, Admiral Nomura, to learn his opinion. "They mean it, they're warning you," said Nomura, "if you go north of the 38th Parallel they'll come in. They'll have to do that to save face, to live up to their words."

Burke asked if, under the circumstances, Nomura thought the Americans should invade North Korea. Nomura said, "Yes. You've got to defeat them now. They started this war, so they have to be punished."

"That was my first indication," Burke later said, "that China would come into the war."

Despite China's verbal threats and reports of Chinese soldiers south of the Yalu River,

NA 80-G-422081

Coffee and cigarettes seem the order of the day as commanding officers of the ships in Mine Division 31 discuss minesweeping operations off Wonsan on 26 October 1950.

NA 80-G-422073

With mines cleared from the narrow approach lane, LST 1048 *prepares to disgorge its LVTs packed with Marines. With no enemy opposition, the Marines would soon be ashore.*

MacArthur's huge intelligence staff continued to believe that the Chinese neither were in North Korea in numbers nor were they about to enter the war. Joy had but a handful of intelligence officers, who had to depend upon the Army for raw data, but they interpreted the data far differently—the Chinese were coming. His instincts conditioned by Nomura, Burke thought so as well. As they would throughout the Chinese offensive, Joy and Burke relayed to Sherman and Radford the manic-depressive atmosphere at MacArthur's headquarters tempered with their own steady assessments. Key messages

NA 80-G-439869

A blinding snowstorm on 15 November suspends air operations from Philippine Sea *(CV 47). An unusually bitter winter set in early for the allies at sea and on land.*

NA 80-G-K11765

Task Force 77 commander, Rear Admiral Edward C. Ewen (second from right), chats with Navy Secretary Francis P. Matthews and two pilots who have just returned to Philippine Sea *from a strike mission over North Korea.*

(paraphrased) from Admiral Joy are summarized below:

October 3rd : MacArthur will issue ultimatum to North Korea in a few days.

October 8th: MacArthur's staff working on plans for occupation of Korea (something of little interest to Joy). . . . Although end of war appears near, there may be enough strength left in North Korea to effect unpleasant resistance. They are beginning to fight as if they expect appreciable help from Manchuria, General Walker notwithstanding.

October 14th: Herewith the future ground phases. a) Eighth Army will attack Pyongyang from the south and X Corps from the west. b) When they merge X Corps will be dissolved and return to Japan. c) Immediately when war is over Eighth Army will be withdrawn and

NA 80-G-423495

On 18 November 1950, Task Force 77 Skyraiders from carrier Leyte *(CV 32) attacked the Yalu River bridges, dropping three spans of the highway bridge connecting Sinuiju, North Korea, with the Manchurian city of Antung. The Joint Chiefs of Staff strictly prohibited pilots from penetrating Manchurian airspace, creating tactical problems for the aviators.*

United Nations occupation commander established. As many United States troops as feasible will be withdrawn leaving minimum military.

MacArthur's apprehension became evident in early November as more Chinese entered North Korea.

November 7th [morning]: We estimate that the situation 10 days ago was not as rosy as pictured and now not as depressing as Army intelligence states, although it is not now good.

November 7th [evening]: Discussed situation with General Hickey [MacArthur's acting chief of staff]. I believe recent dispatches from MacArthur may be misinterpreted as unduly alarming. My estimate of the situation follows: . . . There are quite a few targets in North Korea if we can find them and apparently the Chinese will send more over if we run short. The Army still has potential to knock hell out of as many Chinese communists as they want to push into the hopper. The Air Force and the Navy can help the Army do it.

November 11th: Plans are being made for Eighth Army to attack on November 15th. Bridges over Yalu should be down by then. X Corps appears to us sailors to be over-extended and with regiments so far separated in mountainous country they lack mutual support. Also no reserve. If enemy attacks any regiment with strength there will be great need for lots of air support for which Struble is prepared.

Struble and his Seventh Fleet carriers were indeed needed to support the Army. After discussions with the Army and Air Force, Joy told Struble what to expect.

Notified General Hickey that the carriers were going up to fight and not to act only as a reservoir if needed, which was concurred in. General Hickey stated not for dissemination that North Korea outside U.N. control was to be destroyed since back of enemy resistance must be broken quickly. I suggested

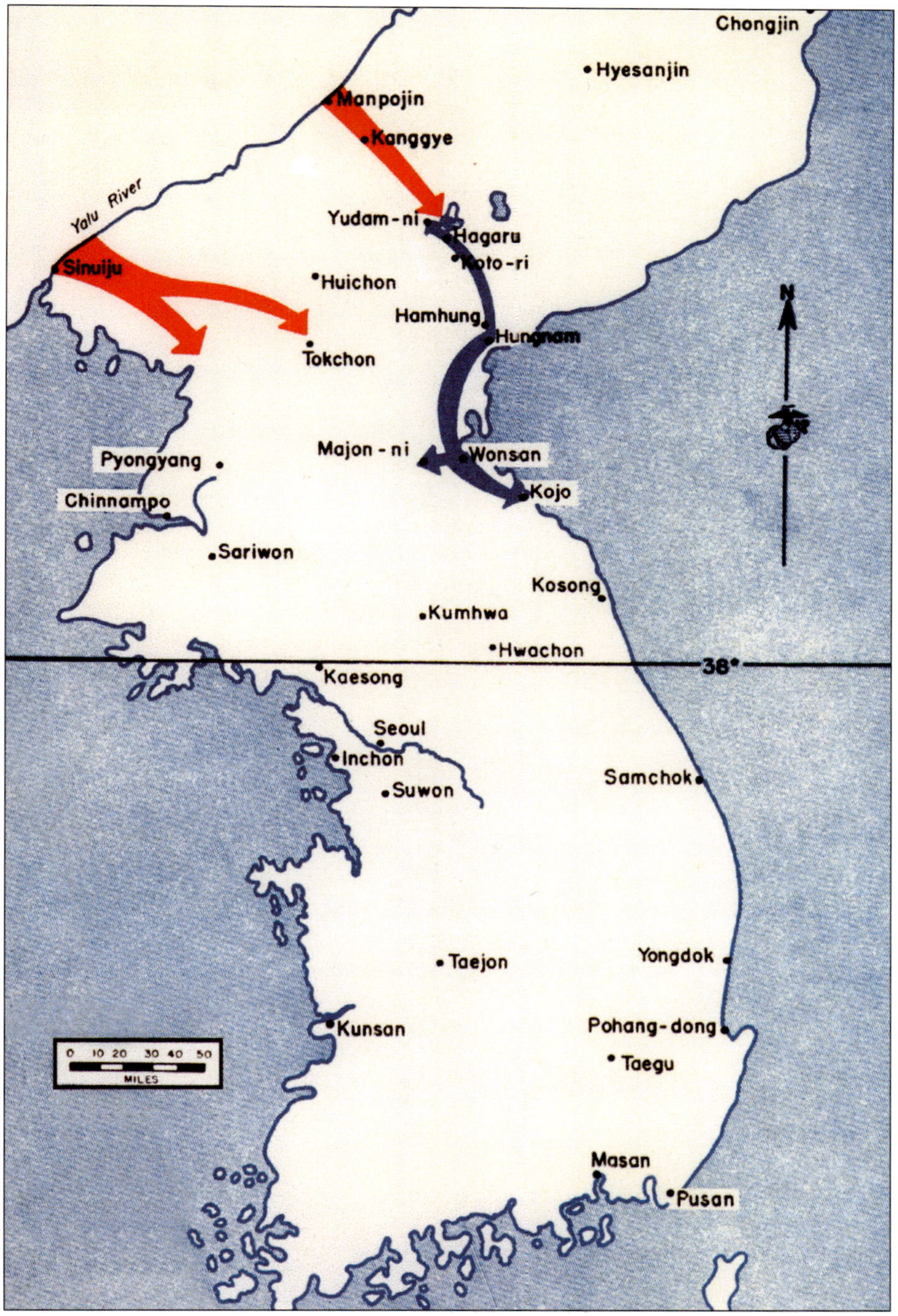

The red arrows track the Chinese and North Korean advance from the Yalu River during the enemy attempt to encircle the outnumbered UN forces in November-December 1950.

Courtesy U.S. Marine Corps

NA-80G-K-11755

A giant floating crane and the wing of a F9F Panther frame the carrier Princeton's *(CV 37) superstructure as she takes on supplies in Sasebo, Japan, before returning to the Korean combat area in early December 1950.*

> however that power plants and dams not be destroyed without specific orders of MacArthur. More power to you.

Predictably the JCS ordered MacArthur not to attack the Yalu bridges, then relented after his outraged protests, with the provision that Navy and Air Force pilots were not to fly over Chinese territory nor fire on any targets on the north bank of the Yalu. Rear Admiral Edward C. Ewen, commanding the carrier task force (Task Force 77), was furious, for Chinese antiaircraft batteries on the north bank could fire with impunity on his aircraft attacking the bridges. The suicidal rules of engagement remained in effect notwithstanding.

The need to take out the bridges seemed about to be overtaken by events, for by 23 November MacArthur and his staff had regained their confidence. The Eighth Army in the east resumed its offensive, and it would, they predicted, be at the Yalu in two weeks. The 2d Infantry Division would be withdrawn early to the United States if, as Joy put it, "North Korea becomes a pushover." The Marines and the 24th Infantry Division would follow shortly. The occupation plan was almost ready but not approved, for it was "subject to radical changes," Joy concluded.

"Army still buoyantly hopeful war will be over by Christmas," Joy reported on 26 November. "General MacArthur flew over North Korean Army and near Yalu and is optimistic, but there may be sneakers left in unpredictable oriental war. [Burke and I] have cautious but hopeful outlook." Burke prudently had begun to put transport ships in reserve, foreseeing the possibility that the troops and their equipment might well have to be evacuated if the Chinese struck in force.

Joy and Burke realized the next day that something was dreadfully wrong when, just past midnight on 28 November, they received a warning from a lieutenant commander attached to the 24th Infantry Division. "Big Ears report for your eyes only. Situation here becoming critical. Borders on desperate. Could result demand for evacuation plan Chinnampo [west coast of North Korea] or further north. Request for all Navy air may be made and needed. Not my business but you should know." Acting on the warning from the front, Joy and Burke immediately alerted Struble and Doyle. "Rumor may be unfounded," they concluded, "but be ready for drastic redeployment."

Army communicators in I Corps had encrypted and sent the message, so Joy and Burke had reason to believe that the front line troops hoped that Joy would take the warning directly to MacArthur, which he did. Their concern was well founded: MacArthur's staff confirmed that the Chinese army had attacked in great force during the night of 27–28 November and assessed the situation as serious but not yet critical. "However," they advised Sherman and Radford, "we are preparing for drastic action nevertheless. Army should be able to hold."

Joy watched developments unfold throughout the 28th, and late in the day reported to Sherman and Radford that the ground situation was not good. MacArthur and his staff were depressed, he said, yet Joy saw no immediate danger of a collapse or need for evacuation, for he still had faith in the fighting ability of the Marines and soldiers. But the Eighth Army and X Corps were fighting separate and uncoordinated battles, and for them to survive Joy thought that the Army had to fix its command structure and corps boundaries.

◆ ◆ ◆

Within the next 48 hours, Joy and Burke fully grasped the gravity of the unfolding disaster. General Hickey on the morning of 30 November called a conference of his chief staff officers, the Air Force, and Burke. He was not an alarmist, said Hickey, but there comes a time when facts have to be faced, and the things he feared might happen, had happened. It was apparent to him that the Chinese intended to commit all their forces to battle in an attempt to annihilate totally the United Nations forces. It was quite possible evacuations would be necessary on both coasts, and that some large troop concentrations might not be able to fight their way to the coasts.

He asked Burke about the rate of possible evacuations.

Burke replied that the Navy had already prepared an evacuation plan for either or both Inchon and Wonsan on short notice. Hickey warned him to keep the information concerning an evacuation in the highest secrecy, but to take preparatory steps without revealing their intentions. "Steady on," said Burke as he left the Army doomsayers.

Joy and Burke afterward pondered what Hickey had said and what they, in turn, had to pass on to their bosses in Washington and Pearl Harbor. As naval officers reporting upon their Army counterparts engaged in a battle to survive, theirs was a ticklish role. Were they competent (or perhaps presumptuous) to judge what was happening in chaotic battles on Korean soil hundreds of miles away from Tokyo? And would they, if roles hypothetically were reversed, have felt that generals were privileged to judge the employment of naval forces engaged in a decisive fleet action?

But Joy and Burke did not have time for reflecting. They had to tell Sherman and Radford *something*,

NA 80-G-424768

Left to right, Rear Admiral James H. Doyle; Major General Field Harris, Commanding General, 1st Marine Aircraft Wing; and Lieutenant General Lemuel C. Shepherd Jr., Commanding General, Fleet Marine Force, Pacific, meet at Yonpo airfield on 8 December. These leaders discuss the withdrawal of allied troops from Chosin and their seaborne evacuation from the port of Hungnam.

Courtesy Naval Aviation News

A Corsair, barely visible through the rising smoke, has just bombed enemy troops, permitting the exhausted Marines to continue their arduous march to the sea. Navy and Marine Corps close air support was critical to the Marines' reaching the evacuation port of Hungnam.

and soon, and what they ultimately reported had to be so phrased as not to cause Washington, already jittery from MacArthur's alarums, to over react. Well, Sherman and Radford were solid; they could handle harsh truths. With Joy beside him, Burke took a blank message pad and began to write.

It was clear to them, Burke wrote, that the mood in MacArthur's headquarters was defeatist. The Army wanted to cut and run to another Dunkirk. A hasty evacuation suggested by Hickey was possible, but what of those Army troops that Hickey had said were isolated inland? Were they to be abandoned? The Army could hold on, they reckoned, if there was but one overall commander (the dual command of Walker and Almond prevented coordination and cooperation), and if that commander concentrated his forces across the peninsula from Chinnampo to Wonsan where the Navy could provide flanking support through the ports. (Burke had suggested this earlier to the Army staff but had been ignored as being out of his realm.)

Now they made their most compelling point to Sherman and Radford. An evacuation of the peninsula would be disastrous to America's international interests.

> If an evacuation becomes necessary the war from then on will be a purely naval war. If this happens our Army will be demoralized and it will be a long time before we again venture into land warfare. Realities dictate that the position of the United States in the Pacific from now on may be determined by the Navy's capabilities in a maritime warfare. [We] are prepared for this contingency but it is

desirable that such forces as are trained and available be readied for onward routing in case this evacuation takes a long time or we lose much shipping in the process.

Parenthetically they added that the Air Force was planning to attack targets in Manchuria and had asked for naval participation. The Navy responded it would not be an appropriate use of carrier aircraft, which were needed to support the troops fighting for their lives. The chasm between the Navy and the Air Force on the proper use of tactical air could not have been more evident.

Even before reporting to Sherman and Radford, Joy had sent a "Flash" precedence message for admirals only, just before midnight on the 30th. It directed Struble and Doyle to put their ships on two-hour notice and otherwise prepare for probable troop evacuations, warning them to maintain secrecy in order not "to jeopardize the Army's present intentions." In other words, Joy knew that the Army was at the breaking point, and he feared they might bolt and run to the nearest port if they knew ships were on the way. All of the senior flag officers in contact with the Army shared this concern, and collectively they would try by various means to stiffen the Army resolve to fight it out on the Korean peninsula.

Joy revealed these naval preparations in a report to Sherman and Radford late at night on 1 December, which disclosed that the Army was ready to abandon Korea and withdraw to Japan. MacArthur was apparently in seclusion and no longer given to the histrionics that

NA 80-G-430078

As the war progressed, Struble, seen here in his flagship **Missouri**, *felt increasingly isolated from the center of action. Doyle complained to Joy that Struble had interfered at Inchon and refused to work under him at Hungnam. Joy acceded to Doyle's demand.*

marked his performance before Inchon. "The Army has been informed," Joy reported, "that we believe they can hold the bridgeheads at both Inchon and Hungnam indefinitely with the help of naval gunfire support and naval air as well as Air Force air and Army tanks and artillery. They agree with us and they recognize the power we can provide."

Joy's next paragraph was stunning.

The Army believes however that the Chinese communists have made a decision to throw in all the manpower necessary to overrun Korea regardless of the after effect this will have on a Third World War. The Army believes too that if the United States attacks Manchuria or China that it would not be advisable to hold a bridgehead in Korea but that it would be preferable to return our troops to Japan to defend the Japanese Islands. [Emphasis added. Apparently MacArthur felt that China was not unwilling to precipitate a third world war. He seems to have reasoned that bombing Manchuria and China, which he advocated, would not help the situation in Korea but would accelerate the start of a third world war, which he would fight out behind the barricades in Japan. The old general had lost his senses.]

The success of establishing a dependable perimeter is dependent upon our ability to disengage some forces for sufficient time to establish defensive positions and supplies. So far this fundamental requirement had not been met by Eighth Army and may not be possible by X Corps. . . .

Am holding 40 cargo ships in ballast as they become available. Used 25 for 2 divisions so 40 should do the trick.

We do not want to be alarmist and for guidance this report is more optimistic than the outlook presented at Army headquarters. Army generals Hickey and Wright are conservative men who know their job and have a pretty good grasp of naval power. Their opinions are more pessimistic than this report but they too believe we can hold a beachhead with naval help.

Radford read Joy's reports and, taking a global view, believed the Chinese attack presaged even more serious attacks elsewhere, perhaps the third world war that MacArthur seemed to be accepting. Naturally, Joy focused solely on Korea and had requested that the attack carrier *Boxer* (CV 21) and other ships be dispatched to the theater. The situation, he explained to Radford, was not as bad as the Army was reporting, and he did not intend to be alarmist; nonetheless, the ground forces needed all the air and naval gunfire support the Navy could provide.

NA 80-G-K-11768

Cruiser **Saint Paul** *(CA 73) secures after firing on targets during the December 1950 evacuation of Hungnam. The 5-inch gun mount of the amphibious force flagship* **Mount McKinley** *(AGC 7) is in the foreground.*

Radford phoned Joy to assess exactly what kind of naval reinforcements were needed and when. Radford already had sent nearly everything he could to Korea; he could scratch for a few more ships, but if he did it would "aggravate the overall unsatisfactory readiness for a general emergency which is a major concern at this time. This readiness has progressively declined because of the continuing demand of the *limited emergency* [emphasis added] in Korea." After talking with Joy, Radford felt that the situation while serious was not as grave as he had first supposed. He told Joy he regretted he could not send reinforcements but "trusted that he would understand that the very emergency which caused him so much concern increased the probability of a general emergency for which the whole Pacific fleet must be prepared."

Radford's concerns of a war elsewhere ultimately proved unfounded, but at the time such perceptions conditioned the thinking of the top leaders. When Radford told Sherman of his conversation with Joy, Sherman directed the Pacific Fleet commander to keep *Bataan* (CVL 29) and *Bairoko* (CVE 115) available to Joy. The Chinese attack may have seemed a "limited emergency" to Radford, but Sherman saw clearly that the Navy had to do everything in its power to support MacArthur and keep the Army and Marine Corps in Korea. Moreover, Sherman had to ensure that whatever the outcome of the Chinese attack, no one could ever find cause to blame the Navy for not having done all in its power to support MacArthur. God help the Navy if MacArthur ever had reason to make that kind of accusation.

Burke saw first hand the defeatism shown by some elements of the Army. "[W]e could have held the Chinese ground forces," he later said, "but as it turned out we didn't, we couldn't."

It got to be pretty desperate. The Chinese knocked the hell out of the Army on the west coast. The 2nd Infantry Division

USN 434918

Cruiser **Rochester** *(CA 124) stands ready at Hungnam to cover the evacuation of UN troops. Navy and Marine air support as well as gunfire support kept the enemy from interfering while troops were loaded.*

came back routed. They lost their elementary wisdom of how to fight a war. They kept to the road instead of putting out flanking detachments, and, of course, the Chinese overwhelmed them.

I talked to the division commander as soon as he got back to Japan. He had been sent back in disgrace . . . he didn't know what had happened to him. He cried, a major general, sat there and cried, telling me what he thought happened. He just lost command of his outfit. He lost his own ability to think, and the first thing a man's got to do when his force is knocked to pieces is to gather them together and get them to fight, or he loses them all.

He didn't do that. We just had the hell kicked out of us.

Joy had issued contingency plans on 13 November for emergency evacuations should they be necessary, and O. P. Smith had told Doyle he intended to slow the rate of advance as his 1st Marine Division neared the Yalu. Almond urged him to move faster, but Smith sensed a Chinese ambush and proceeded cautiously and deliberately. "Thank God he did," Doyle later wrote, "for on 27 November the Marines ran into massive Chinese Communist formations that would have gobbled up a dispersed division piecemeal. As it was, upon receipt of orders to return to Hungnam, the 1st Marine Division formed a legion which marched through the enemy like Caesar through Gaul, destroying seven Chinese divisions and ending

NH 97060

Marines board **Bayfield** *(APA 33) for the evacuation from North Korea. In the fight to reach Hungnam, the Marines had badly damaged the Communists' capabilities, but the war would drag on for another three years.*

the Communist offensive capability in eastern North Korea."

◆ ◆ ◆

Once Doyle foresaw that an evacuation at Hungnam was probable, he went to Joy with furrowed brow and a presumptuous demand. "Doyle complained to me," Joy later wrote, "that at Inchon Struble was continually in his hair and interfering with his exercise of command." Doyle insisted that Struble, his nominal senior by a full rank, be kept clear of Hungnam and that Doyle have absolute command of the operation. Joy could have told Doyle to follow orders, but perhaps he was unsure whether Doyle would obey, so deep-seated was his antipathy. We will never know. Joy acceded to Doyle's demand. Joy later explained: "As Doyle was more valuable to the success of Hungnam than Struble I thought it best to keep them separated as much as possible." Struble would of course object bitterly, but such was the urgency of the evacuation that Joy was willing to take the heat.

This was the third time that Joy had denied Struble the command prerogatives he felt his rank deserved, the first at Pohang-dong at the beginning of the war, then over the Wonsan minesweepers. Joy's decision regarding Hungnam contradicted the policy he had received earlier from Sherman, who had insisted that Struble be in overall command of amphibious operations when carriers and fleet support were involved. But Sherman, too, could not afford to affront Doyle, who was indispensable, and Struble was not. Doyle got his way, but Hungnam would be his last hurrah, and his finest hour.

When Joy met with Doyle at Hungnam to discuss the forthcoming evacuation, he was accompanied by Lieutenant General Lemuel C. Shepherd Jr., who commanded the Pacific Fleet Marine Force and was the senior Marine in the Pacific. Doyle was pleased when Shepherd remained with him when Joy returned to Tokyo. "Insofar as I knew," Doyle later wrote,

> Shepherd remained simply as an observer and to give whatever advice and assistance he could. Thus it was with considerable surprise that I learned 25 years after the withdrawal that [Radford] had directed that if the evacuation was not moving

NA 80-G-K-11772

Destroyer Massey *(DD 778) steams astern of Admiral Doyle's flagship,* Mount McKinley *(AGC 7), from which he directed the epic evacuation of over 100,000 UN troops and 91,000 Korean refugees from the port of Hungnam.* Massey *provided protective cover by shelling enemy concentrations in the area until amphibious forces completed the evacuation on 24 December. She then turned her guns on the port facilities, helping to demolish them.*

> properly under me, command would shift to General Shepherd. This arrangement apparently had the agreement of both Joy and Shepherd. . . . [I]f I had known of Radford's instructions at the time, I would have been insulted, because to me those orders cast doubt on my competence to command the withdrawal. Fortunately, I knew nothing of the scheme. Certainly neither Turner Joy, who was my friend, nor Lem Shepherd, one of the Lord's own, would have ever taken advantage of the deal proposed.

The JCS ordered MacArthur to evacuate the X Corps at Hungnam in order to concentrate allied forces in South Korea. The evacuation began on 9 December under Doyle's command. In terms of military operations, a withdrawal from the battlefield while under attack from an aggressive enemy is hazardous and potentially disastrous. To prevent a rout the withdrawing forces must remain cohesive and disciplined, moving to the rear with measured steps. While some of the Army staffs were willing to leave equipment and supplies behind to expedite the evacuation, Doyle would not hear of it. Everything would be loaded at Hungnam and taken away.

The United States Navy had never evacuated such a large body of troops under fire, only landed them, so Doyle and his planners had no precedents. But it was clear that the Chinese had to be kept at a distance from the port so that the shipping could safely enter and embark passengers and cargo. Doyle employed Marine and carrier aircraft, naval gunfire, and artillery to saturate the approaching Chinese with overwhelming firepower, while rear guard troops fought off any enemy forces that got through the barrage. The payoff was an uninterrupted, systematic embarkation.

The 3d Infantry Division was still fighting as a rear guard when Almond came aboard Doyle's flagship with his headquarters on 19 December. Doyle greeted Almond and looked him in the eye. "You understand, General," said Doyle, "that those troops are now under my command."

Years later Doyle told this tale with wicked relish. "When I told Almond that," he grinned, "you had to hold him down?"

On Christmas Eve day the last of the troops boarded the ships and Doyle's force sailed. Timed demolition charges and naval gunfire then destroyed the port facilities. When the Chinese army finally entered Hungnam they found it a barren city. Doyle had taken out everything of value: one Marine and two Army divisions and a ROK corps totaling 105,000 personnel; 17,500 tanks and other vehicles; and 350,000 tons of cargo. In addition, 91,000 Korean civilian refugees were rescued.

The Navy took the UN troops to Pusan, enabling them to survive and fight another day.

Epilogue

FORREST SHERMAN died of a heart attack on 22 July 1951 at age 54, while serving as Chief of Naval Operations. He had been CNO for only 33 months.

Arthur Radford continued as Commander in Chief, Pacific Command, and Commander in Chief, Pacific Fleet, until President Dwight D. Eisenhower appointed him chairman of the Joint Chiefs of Staff in June 1953. He received a Gold Star in lieu of a third Distinguished Service Medal for exceptionally meritorious service during the Korean War. Radford served two terms as JCS chairman before retiring in August 1957. He died in 1973 at age 77.

C. Turner Joy served as Commander Naval Forces, Far East until May 1952. In July 1951, he served concurrently as Senior United Nations Delegate at the Korean Armistice Conference at Panmunjom and Kaesong, a bitterly frustrating task that he wrote about in his book *How Communists Negotiate*. He received the Army Distinguished Service Cross and the Navy Distinguished Service Medal for exceptionally meritorious service in relation to the Korean War. He returned to the United States and served as superintendent of the U.S. Naval Academy before retiring in 1954 with a promotion to full admiral in recognition of his World War II combat awards. He died in 1956 at age 61.

Arthur Struble was relieved as Commander Seventh Fleet in March 1951 and served in a variety of high command and staff positions on the U.S. East Coast. He received the Army Distinguished Service Cross and a Gold Star in lieu of a second Navy Distinguished Service Medal for exceptionally meritorious service in Korea. He retired in 1956 and received a promotion to full admiral in recognition of his World War II combat awards. He died in 1983 at age 88.

James Doyle was relieved as CTF 90 in early 1951 and received the Distinguished Service Medal for exceptionally meritorious service in Korea. He then served eight months as president of the Board of Inspection and Survey. For the final 18 months of his active service, he chaired the Joint Amphibious Board, but to what extent he influenced the development of amphibious doctrine in that capacity is unclear. At his retirement on 1 November 1953, he was promoted to vice admiral in recognition of his World War II combat awards. He practiced law in retirement and died in 1981 at age 83.

Arleigh Burke continued as deputy chief of staff on Joy's staff until he returned to sea as Commander Cruiser Division 5 off Korea. After a few short weeks in command he was appointed to serve with Joy in Panmunjom and Kaesong as a United Nations Delegate at the Korean Armistice Conference, a job he despised for its lack of success. He received a Gold Star in lieu of a third Legion of Merit from the Navy and an Oak Leaf Cluster from the Army in lieu of a fourth Legion of Merit, both for exceptionally meritorious conduct in Korea. He returned to Washington in December 1951 as the director of the CNO's Strategic Plans Division. He went back to sea as a cruiser division commander and then became Commander Destroyer Force, Atlantic Fleet. In August 1955, Burke bypassed 91 flag officers senior to himself when he was chosen to be Chief of Naval Operations. A four-star admiral, he served in that capacity for a record three appointments totaling six years before retiring in 1961. The Navy named a destroyer class in Burke's honor while he was living in retirement. He died in 1996 at age 94.

About the Author

Commander Thomas B. Buell, USN (Ret.), is a distinguished author, scholar, and military historian. A graduate of the U.S. Naval Academy and the Naval Postgraduate School, he stood first in his class at the Naval War College. His writing began with professional articles for the U.S. Naval Institute *Proceedings,* where he later served on the Naval Institute editorial board. While on the staff of the Naval War College he wrote *The Quiet Warrior: A Biography of Admiral Raymond A. Spruance,* which was copublished by Little, Brown and the Naval Institute Press. Following command at sea, he taught military and naval history at the United States Military Academy and wrote *Master of Sea Power: A Biography of Fleet Admiral Ernest J. King,* again copublished by Little, Brown and the Naval Institute Press, and a main selection of the Military Book Club.

Both books received the Alfred Thayer Mahan Award for Literary Achievement and the Samuel Eliot Morison Award for Naval Literature. *The Quiet Warrior* has been in continuous print for 27 years, most recently as a selection of the Naval Institute's "Classics of Naval Literature" series, where it has been joined by *Master of Sea Power.*

Tom Buell has lectured and presented papers at universities, foundations, and such service institutions as the Naval Academy, the Naval War College, the National War College, the Army War College, the Army Command and Staff College, the Air War College, the Royal Military College of Canada, and the Marine Corps Command and Staff College.

He is now a writer-in-residence at the University of North Carolina at Chapel Hill and is a guest lecturer in history at UNC and Duke. His most recent work is *The Warrior Generals: Combat Leadership in the Civil War* (New York: Crown, 1997), which is an alternate selection of the Military Book Club. His next book, *The Sea Warrior Trilogy,* will be published by Oxford University Press.

Sources

Archival Collections

Office of the Chief of Naval Operations. Microfilm message files, reels TS–53–62. Operational Archives (OA), Naval Historical Center (NHC), Washington Navy Yard, DC.

Burke, Arleigh A. Oral History, vols. 1 and 3. U.S. Naval Institute Oral History Collection, Annapolis, MD.

Cagle, Malcolm W., and Frank A. Manson Papers. OA, NHC.

Doyle, James lecture, 14 March 1974, Naval War College, Newport, RI.

Heinl, Robert D. Papers. Marine Corps University Archives, Quantico, VA.

Smith, Oliver P. Papers. Marine Corps University Archives, Quantico, VA.

Struble, Arthur D. Papers. OA, NHC.

Books

Barlow, Jeffrey G. *Revolt of the Admirals: The Fight for Naval Aviation, 1945–1950.* Washington: Naval Historical Center, 1994.

Cagle, Malcolm W., and Frank A. Manson. *The Sea War in Korea.* Annapolis: Naval Institute Press, 1957.

Field, Jr., James A. *History of United States Naval Operations: Korea.* Washington: GPO, 1962.

Heinl, Jr., Robert D. *Victory at High Tide: The Inchon-Seoul Campaign.* Annapolis: Nautical & Aviation Co. of America, 1979.

Jurika, Stephen, Jr., ed. *From Pearl Harbor to Vietnam: The Memoirs of Admiral Arthur W. Radford.* Stanford: Hoover Institution Press, 1980.

Manchester, William. *American Cæsar.* Boston: Little, Brown, 1978.

Potter, E. B. *Admiral Arleigh Burke.* New York: Random House, 1990.

Reynolds, Clark G. "Forrest Percival Sherman." In *The Chiefs of Naval Operations,* edited by Robert William Love Jr. Annapolis: Naval Institute Press, 1980.

Rosenberg, David Alan. "Arleigh Albert Burke." In *The Chiefs of Naval Operations,* edited by Robert William Love Jr. Annapolis: Naval Institute Press, 1980.

Articles

Chisholm, Donald. "Negotiated Joint Command Relationships: Korean War Amphibious Operations, 1950." *Naval War College Review* (Spring 2000).

Doyle, James H., and Arthur J. Mayer. "December 1950 at Hungnam." U.S. Naval Institute *Proceedings* (April 1979).

Suggested Reading

The Navy Department Library at the Washington Navy Yard lists some 35 entries for American naval operations in the Korean War, 1950–1953. Most are memoirs of service in individual ships or squadrons and tell little about the naval leaders who are the protagonists in this monograph. I suggest seven works for reading, with the understanding that most of my research material was from primary, unpublished sources. The Cagle-Manson and Field histories are available on CD-ROM from the Naval Historical Center.

The Sea War in Korea, written by two active duty naval officers, Malcolm W. Cagle and Frank A. Manson, was the first complete work on the history of naval operations in Korea. The authors relied mainly on interviews of participants and what they saw for themselves as most of the relevant documents were still classified. Published only four years after the war actively concluded, their work necessarily lacks historical perspective. The authors asked key participants to read the drafts, a great mistake, for certain senior officers considered that they could veto whatever they disagreed with. Struble insisted that his point of view be reflected in the text, and the authors generally acceded. For all these reasons this book is somewhat out of date, but it can still be read as introductory material.

James A. Field Jr.'s *History of United States Naval Operations: Korea* is the official Navy Department history. Field was a professional historian of great competence, and his writing reflects independent, critical thought sometimes not found in "official" histories. He was, however, handicapped by not being allowed access to Top Secret materials (see "Blue Flag Messages," p. 12). Moreover, he asked senior participants to comment on the manuscript, so Struble's version of events gets more attention than it should. This book nonetheless remains the best reference available on naval operations in the first six months of the war.

Stephen Juricka's *From Pearl Harbor to Vietnam: The Memoirs of Admiral Arthur W. Radford* is the edited version of Radford's considerable memoirs written after his retirement from naval service. Regrettably, Radford was reticent about the Korean War and not much can be learned about his role from this source. Taken as a whole, however, this book informs the reader about Radford's character and personality.

The Chiefs of Naval Operations, edited by Robert W. Love Jr., is the only source where, in but a single chapter by Clark Reynolds, one can learn something about Forrest Sherman. He died prematurely of a heart attack while in office and left few official papers.

E. B. Potter's *Admiral Arleigh Burke* is an abbreviated biography based largely upon Burke's oral history. The great bulk of the work covers Burke's career through World War II, and the book largely runs out of steam covering Burke's career after 1945. Nonetheless, it is the only piece of literature on Burke in Korea other than two paragraphs in the chapter on Burke by David Alan Rosenberg in *The Chiefs of Naval Operations.*

Donald Chisholm's, "Negotiated Joint Command Relationships: Korean War Amphibious Operations, 1950," *Naval War College Review* (Spring 2000) is the only up-to-date work on the naval commanders and was the genesis for this monograph.

Jeffrey G. Barlow's *Revolt of the Admirals: The Fight for Naval Aviation, 1945–1950,* written by a Navy historian, covers the postwar, high-level Navy–Air Force infighting over the role of the naval service, particularly its aviation component, in the new national security structure. Based on extensive primary sources from Navy, Air Force, and JCS files and on selected interviews with senior naval officers, this book provides an unparalleled look at the personal interaction of important Navy flag officers such as Arthur Radford, Arthur Struble, and Forrest Sherman in the years leading up to the Korean War.

ISBN 0-16-051080-5

90000

9 780160 510809